A courageous life-story of God's redeeming lov̶ ̶̶̶̶̶̶̶̶̶̶g ̶p̶o̶w̶e̶r̶. ̶K̶a̶t̶h̶r̶y̶n weaves the tapestry of her life with such vulnerability and transparency.

Angie Gray
Transformational Life Coach

The experiences of the Author will encourage many to overcome and assist in growing their faith. Once you start reading you will not be able to put this book down!

—J. Lynn Kronk, PhD
Co-Founder of Lifestyle Game Changers

What a great reminder that we are *all* beautiful works of art in process of becoming signature masterpieces! Anyone who currently knows Kathryn would never guess her origin of hardship and trauma. Kathryn is a testimony to everything she has communicated in this book. The application of this revelation-power communicated in her book, is undoubtedly why I would have never imagined the origins of her story. She has allowed the Father to show her the truth, "Behind Enemy Lies,"and has allowed Him to take what was meant to kill and destroy every part of her destiny, and instead catapult her into her calling of communicating truth through written word. This book is the first of many, and I look forward to reading every word of revelatory truth that the Father writes through her. Kathryn, you are a signature masterpiece. The value of every masterpiece is in the signature. He wrote His name all over your story.

—Ashley Dawson

Behind Enemy Lies is riveting and kept me on my toes. Knowing Kathryn now, I would never have guessed she endured all the hard things she shares about in this book. I am amazed to see how the love of God has healed her. I believe Kathryn's story will help others find freedom. *Behind Enemy Lies* was a powerful depiction of the awesome God we serve. Thank you for listening to God when he said for you to stand tall, be brave and tell the world what you went through so that others could see Him.

—Kelley Spindle

I cannot say enough about this book! Kathryn has written this very hard story of her life with excellence. It captivated me from the minute I started reading! Look what the Lord has done for you!

—Pam Crane

KATHRYN ROSE MAY

BEHIND ENEMY LIES

Abuse, Deception &
A Journey from
Darkness to Light

A MEMOIR

MILK & HONEY BOOKS

Scripture quotations marked (ESV) are from The ESV® Bible (The Holy Bible, English Standard Version®), copyright © 2001 by Crossway, a publishing ministry of Good News Publishers. Used by permission. All rights reserved.

Scripture quotations marked (MSG) are taken from THE MESSAGE, copyright © 1993, 2002, 2018 by Eugene H. Peterson. Used by permission of NavPress, represented by Tyndale House Publishers. All rights reserved.

Scripture quotations marked (NLT) are taken from the Holy Bible, New Living Translation, copyright ©1996, 2004, 2015 by Tyndale House Foundation. Used by permission of Tyndale House Publishers, a Division of Tyndale House Ministries, Carol Stream, Illinois 60188. All rights reserved.

Scripture quotations marked TPT are from The Passion Translation®. Copyright © 2017, 2018 by Passion & Fire Ministries, Inc. Used by permission. All rights reserved. ThePassionTranslation.com.

Cover Photo: Deposit Photos

This book is available at: www.milkandhoneybooks.com and other online retailers
Reach us on the Internet: www.milkandhoneybooks.com

Print ISBN 13: 978-1-953000-14-9
Ebook ISBN 13: 978-1-953000-15-6

For Worldwide Distribution

The stories in this book reflect the author's recollection of events. Some names, locations, and identifying characteristics have been changed to protect the privacy of those depicted. Dialogue has been re-created from memory.

DEDICATION

For every woman who believes she is unworthy, unloved, and
unseen. I pray as you read the pages of my story you will see
yourself in it and know the truth and the truth will set you free.
That you will know if He did it for me, He will do it for you and
if He did it once, He can do it again.

He heals the brokenhearted and binds up their wounds.
Psalm 147:3

ACKNOWLEDGMENTS

There are so many amazing people who invested time, encouragement, and prayer into the development of this project. Without them I would not have been able to complete this challenging work.

I have to start by thanking my awesome husband, James. From listening, to reading early drafts, to keeping our children entertained so I could edit, to encouraging me to keep going every time I wanted to quit, thank you so much my sweet.

I want to thank my dad, Michael, for being a steady voice of support, giving me confidence to finish and always seeing the best in me. Thank you, Dad, for being brave enough to let me share our story. You're the best!

To all three of my children, Harold Michael, Brianna, and Isaac, who have sacrificed so much mommy time while I completed this important message of hope, healing and forgiveness, you are the best gifts God has given me. Thank you for your understanding. I love you so much.

To my dear friend, Jenny Erlingsson. Thank you for partnering with me to see this baby birthed! Your knowledge and insight as a published author and now publishing house, has been incredible. Thank you for believing in me, sister!

I also want to thank all the countless people who read and re-read portions of my story and helped me with the tedious job of editing.

To those who gave me feedback throughout the writing process, thank you for your sensitivity and encouragement. You are invaluable and I love each one of you.

To all of those who were part of my journey to freedom, leading me to find truth in the Word of God, thank you. My story is possible because of your sacrifice and labor of love.

Most importantly, Jesus Christ. I am eternally grateful to You, my Mighty Warrior, King and Deliverer. To you be all the praise, all the honor and all the glory. Without your comfort I could never have comforted others. Thank you for using all my brokenness and creating something beautiful. Thank you for never giving up on me.

—Kathryn Rose

TABLE OF CONTENTS

INTRODUCTION

My mother named me Kathryn Rose, meaning "pure, flower", the essence of my identity. However, something tragic occurred when I was only a little girl and the "pure" part of my identity was snatched away. With my purity stolen, I was left wilted and broken.

My identity has been under attack since birth. The enemy of my soul, Satan, targeted me because I was a threat. His mission; to destroy all access to the truth of who I was and what I was created for. Satan deployed his plan to separate me from the knowledge of God's love and convince me to trade the truth for a lie that because of what was *done* to me, I was impure, worthless and certainly not beautiful like the flower I was named after.

The word of God says that nothing can separate us from the love of God (Romans 8:39). But, if Satan can separate us from the knowledge of the love of God, he can keep us from living in our full identity as sons and daughters. If he can isolate us behind walls of fear, hopelessness, and pain, we may never realize that we are rescued, redeemed, and restored. We will then live as orphans, feeling unloved, unwanted, and unworthy.

> "But now thus says the Lord, he who created you, O Jacob, he who formed you, O Israel: 'Fear not, for I have redeemed you; I have called you by name, you are mine.'" (Isaiah 43:1 ESV)

He knew me before my conception, fearfully and wonderfully created by God in my mother's womb. Not one part was a mistake. Specific gifts were woven into my DNA with much consideration for who I was to be. A woman chosen for this time and place in history. The plan for my life beautifully laid. Plans to prosper me in all I set out to do and to give me a future in Him that is full of hope and joy. God created me to be courageous, bold, and fierce. Created to be loved, to love, and to advance the Kingdom of Heaven here on Earth. As were you!

You may not know how important you are or that He carefully considered you. Your purpose and place in history thought out well in advance. Maybe it's difficult to conceive how incredibly unique and valuable you are in this moment, but know this: when you took your first breath, all of Heaven rejoiced and all of Hell trembled.

Satan didn't know exactly what God had in mind when He created you; he only knew that if you ever found out, it would be bad for him.

So the battle begins. Flaming arrows and poisonous darts are flung in our direction. Deception is used to pull the scales over our eyes. Fear winds itself tightly to choke out our determination to fight. Seeds of doubt are planted in our mind to sprout a thorny hedge, keeping us from venturing beyond the enemy's lies. Before we have a chance to realize who we really are, the enemy does all he can to tear us down, silence our voice and cloud our mind. He falsely labels us, which leads to an exhausting, mundane, non-threatening life.

This full-on assault from Satan and the army of hell has but one goal: to render us useless to the kingdom of God. If we are bound up in deceit and oppressed by the spirit of fear, we cannot see the truth and therefore have no vision of the life we are meant to live. Isolated with our pain and disappointment, we unknowingly resign ourselves to being prisoners of war. Those meant to be victorious are now victims.

Satan convinces us to follow the crowd down a dark road. It's hard to see clearly and the cliff's edge goes unnoticed until it's too late. Sons and daughters taken out in masses, as we march unknowingly to our demise.

But God calls to us while we shuffle along. "Come to me. Walk this way!"

He jumps around, waving His arms. He shouts over the noise of the thunderous march, "I am here to rescue you! You were meant for more! I love you! Look this way!"

We may not hear Him at first, but He never quits pursuing us. Maybe you have heard this voice calling you out of the dark. Maybe, like me, you have brushed it aside repeatedly as fear slams you in the face and demands that you keep your eyes on the path you were walking. It's not hopeless. Your freedom is just on the other side of the enemy's lies. When we belong to Christ, the enemy never has the last word. We need only listen to the voice calling us toward truth, following it no matter the cost! God's chosen, created children have been called to fight in this spiritual war.

The Word of God tells us to put on the full armor of God so that we can take a stand against the devil's schemes. It also brings to our attention that our war isn't against people, but against the rulers, authorities, and powers of the dark world. We war against spiritual forces of evil.

"Put on God's complete set of armor provided for us, so that you will be protected as you fight against the evil strategies of the accuser! Your hand-to-hand combat is not with human beings, but with the highest principalities and authorities operating in rebellion under the heavenly realms. For they are a powerful class of demon-gods and evil spirits that hold this dark world in bondage." (Ephesians 6:11-12 TPT)

There is a real battle being waged for our soul. But how can we fight what we cannot see? What weapons do we have to gain our freedom? Truth pulls the scales off our eyes so we can begin to see that things are not always what they seem. Since we war against the unseen, we need to ask God for help. We fight with armor given to us by the creator.

When we accept the finished work of the cross, He places on our waist a belt of truth to strengthen us to stand in victory. Jesus said, "I am the way, the truth and the light..." (John 14:6). His truth is our defense against Satan's primary weapon, which is deception. God also gives us a breastplate of righteousness to protect our hearts. Shoes of peace so we are confident in our step. The Commander of the Universe even gives us a shield of faith for protection from the flaming arrows of the evil one. We are given a helmet to protect our minds, salvation is its name and a sword sharper than any other to destroy the enemy... the Word of God (Ephesians 6:13-17).

When I first learned about this invisible battle, I was shocked and unsure. Just knowing about it didn't cause me to throw on my armor and pick up my weapons to fight. I had been trained to be a victim, a slave to the way things were. Deceived, I believed I was not created with any purpose or design.

The plan deployed to destroy my future began with being conditioned to accept a set of beliefs that appeared to be truth. In the mirror I looked into, I could only see a distorted version of who God created me to be. I could not recognize my value or my worth, completely unaware I was being held captive behind enemy lies.

1

WALLS OF FEAR

The enemy never fights fair, attacking at the youngest age possible. I stood in front of my training potty, thrilled that I had just peed where I was supposed to. As I looked at the red urine sitting in the white plastic bowl, I was so proud of myself. Squealing with excitement, I yelled to my mother, "Look mommy I peed Kool-Aid." I remember nothing else about that moment. I only know the man I called dad introduced me to a life of abuse at the age of three.

The abuse I endured throughout my childhood shaped my view of the world, myself and others. This strike by the enemy altered something significant for me relating to my identity. I lived in quiet guilt, hating my existence, and wondering why I was not loved. I accepted the lie that I was damaged goods, broken and worthless.

The Brady Bunch theme song was a tune often hummed by mother from the kitchen. She endearingly called our home a zoo.

With seven children, sometimes it certainly sounded that way. My mother was the picture of poise and grace. She was a real-life June Cleaver, best friend, and an encourager for much of my young life. There was nothing she couldn't do in my eyes! She was strong and steady, never letting us feel her pain or see her broken heart.

You see, our family had a well-kept secret. During the day, we lived a normal life. We had chores and homework. We rode bikes, climbed trees and played in the secluded woods that surrounded us on all four sides. Mother kept the environment peaceful and carefree when we were home alone with her.

However, our daytime reality would often give way to a much darker evening. When we heard the rumble of the blue Ford truck barreling up the dirt driveway, the atmosphere shifted. Mother's relaxed and silly disposition disappeared, replaced by seriousness and tension. Fear gripped my heart and caused me to want to disappear into the same woods I played in earlier that day. When the man I called dad for most of my childhood came in the door, we were hushed and shuffled out of sight. As out of sight as she could get that many children in a three-bedroom trailer.

My mother scurried to get dinner on the table and hoped she played all her cards right so we would have a peaceful night. Sometimes, he didn't like the way the food was cooked and became angry if she didn't wear her long, "little house on the prairie," hand sewn dress with her hair tucked away. He would take her into their bedroom while we heard the thud of her 100-pound body crashing into the wall.

I wasn't sure, but somehow deep down inside I knew that something was wrong with this way of life. As I got older, I often ventured off into the woods hoping a family of bears would take me in and raise me; or better yet, they could just eat me so my life would be over.

My mother suffered the wrath of physical and mental abuse with the evidence of bruises and broken teeth; my abuse was much more hidden.

The house was dark and quiet as everyone fell asleep. I'd lay awake hoping he wouldn't come to me that night. If I wound up tightly enough in my blanket, he wouldn't be able to get in. Maybe this time I could scream. Quietly, I practiced little screams with the covers pulled up to my ears.

It was very secluded in the hills of Missouri, where there were unpaved dead-end roads and miles of trees between neighbors. My screams wouldn't have been heard even if I mustered up the courage. Besides, I knew my mother would come and if she came, he would hurt her.

I lived in fear, knowing he would eventually come to use me but never knowing when. While the crickets were still chirping their symphony outside my window, he took me outside to the big white shed in the backyard. If he didn't come before dawn, I knew at any moment he might decide to take me for a "short drive" or force me to come into the shed to "see something". He never hit me or even spanked me. I was invisible to him unless I was the object of his sick desires.

After each encounter, he threatened me through gritted teeth. "If you ever tell anyone, you're out of here and you'll never see your mother again." At times he resorted to threats, "I will kill her if you tell anyone." Fear was his greatest weapon and power over me.

Terrified, I submitted quietly each time to his command. I never fought. I just closed my eyes and focused on disappearing into the sound of the crickets and frogs on the other side of the door. As I got older, he would introduce me to more of his perverted desires and it became more difficult to disappear into my mind. Pain and embarrassment now gripped my attention and there was no longer an escape. I would choose a knothole in the wood or a leaf swaying in the breeze to focus on, rather than his face, and just wait for it to be over.

Alone, I'd pretend I was strong. I imagined what it might be like to say no, be tough and have control. He wouldn't be allowed to touch me. I would be my own hero. As I dreamed of stopping him, I'd envision my triumph and plan it all out in my mind. The next time he came to me, I would bite him... kick... scream... tell someone! Instead, I froze each time. Over and over again, I failed. I hated him, but even more so, I hated myself.

It became increasingly difficult to live with the hatred, guilt, and anger. I blamed myself for what was happening. I believed it was my fault. I must have done something wrong. I just didn't know what. He never told me he loved me, held my hand, hugged me or even noticed my existence...except for the abuse. Somewhere inside my little girl heart, I resolved I must be broken and unworthy of a father's love. I would never be good enough to earn it and so I began accepting this lie as truth.

I was unlovable.

This belief caused immense self-hatred and overwhelming feelings of worthlessness. I told myself I deserved what was happening to me for being so ugly and weak. I was angry at myself for not being able to stop him. I was angry at doing whatever made me so undeserving of love.

No one ever said I was ugly, weak, unlovable, or worthless with their words. The only words spoken to me by the man I called dad were orders or threats. I perceived I was unloved because of what was happening to me.

I felt if I was a good daughter, I would be accepted and loved. If I was pretty, they would care for me like a valued princess. Since I wasn't treated lovingly, I decided I was unlovable. If I was strong, I could stand up and fight like the movies that played in my mind. I believed I was weak and useless because I always froze in the moments I should have fought.

Every evening I dreaded seeing the headlights of his blue Ford pickup truck come into sight. Butterflies fluttered in my stomach and a boulder of panic sat on my chest.

He was so unpredictable; I never knew what would be in store for the night. I couldn't predict what might set him off and what kind of mood he'd be in. How will it end today? What will he be like when he gets home? There was no expectation of good. I did not know how bad; I just knew it would be.

It wasn't just the fear of what he would do to me. The uncertainty of what kind of wrath my mother or brother might face played a large part in my increasing anxiety. I wished I could disappear. I tried to be invisible, or at least out of sight. If he didn't see me, maybe he wouldn't think about me later.

I was afraid to go anywhere alone while he was home. I stayed as close to mothers' side as I could. She was my "base". When I was with her, he wouldn't touch me. I hid in her shadow as long as I could. When I wasn't with her, I felt as though I were the one protecting her by submitting to his demands.

One of my favorite safe places was her bathroom. I went with her no matter what she was doing. We locked the door and everything else went away. She and I would talk and share stories about our day and for the moment, I was at peace.

One evening after dinner, when I was twelve, my mother informed the household she would go take a shower. As usual, I got up to follow her, only this time I was stopped. The man I called "dad" decided on this rare night that I could not follow her. With that familiar look in his eye, he insisted I needed to go "clean my room."

My room was always clean. I was adamant about keeping things in order. I shared it with three other girls and it had to be in order to have space to move and find things. My heart sank as I pleaded to do it later, but to no avail. I knew why he wanted me to clean my room, but he had never molested me inside the home with everyone awake.

Sometimes I would have to go with him in his truck alone in the middle of the afternoon. However, this time was very different. Didn't he know my brothers and sisters were just in the living room of our three-bedroom trailer? What about my mom?

Trembling inside, I trudged down the hallway to my room. I felt sick. I sat on my already made-up bed and waited. I knew he would come soon, and now more than ever, I wished I could have disappeared. I wanted to run, hide, cry, scream... die.

When the door opened, I remember thinking he hadn't waited very long. Usually, I would do everything within my power to look away from his face, especially the times when he used me. This time, however, I couldn't. There was something strange in his demeanor. He came at me with such a ravenous urgency. It was almost as if he wasn't in control of himself.

As he forced himself on me, he seemed to have an uncontrollable craving that could only be met at that moment. Prior to this time, I never cried when he made me do unspeakable things. I couldn't react in the moment. I would numb my mind or dissociate if I could. I may have cried later but usually, I wouldn't. When I cried, it was because I was so angry thinking about the next time he would come and how I couldn't make him go away. I cried because I was overwhelmed with despair at the thought of my mom coming in the door.

There was no way to distract myself this time. His body was so heavy on mine. I could barely breathe. As I sobbed through shortened breaths, the door flung open and there in the doorway stood my mom, dripping wet and wearing only a towel. Her face was covered with shock and anger. When our eyes locked, I felt a rush of relief and terror all at the same time. I wanted to scream out "Please momma help me," but what would he do? Would he hurt her?

Tears streaming down my cheeks, I kept my eyes on her, waiting for what was to come. My mind raced with every threat he told me would happen if she ever found out.

As quickly as she entered the room, she was gone, cursing him as she slammed the door. He jumped off me as fast as he could.

Grappling to pull up his pants, he followed her down the hall to the other end of the house, where the screaming and fighting escalated.

I was left alone…lying on the bed, half-naked and in shock. It all happened so quickly. How I wished she would have stayed with me, hugged me, let me finally cry all the tears I had been holding back for years. I should have felt rescued; but I felt abandoned, sad, scared, and unsure of what was to come.

Soon I heard the rumble of the blue truck's engine and the sound of tires slinging rocks. I watched from the kitchen window until his taillights were out of sight as he sped down the long driveway. I turned to my mom not knowing what to say. I choked back tears and wished she would call me to her with open arms. Instead, she stared right through me for what felt like an eternity. I broke the silence with one question. "What's going to happen now?"

She sternly replied, "He's gone and never coming back." then sent me off to bed. Was she angry with me? A sudden, greater wave of emotion swept over me. I laid on my pillow and cried until my cheeks felt cramped, my stomach ached, and my eyes felt like they could never open again.

2

THE LIE OF REJECTION

The enemy of our soul watches for opportunities to exploit our weakness. Like a stealthy ninja, he lays crafty traps that aim straight for the pressure points. He then sits back and waits for the perfect storm to arise, hoping to sink us before we can emerge victorious.

The reason the attacks on our identity start early is so that we are less likely to be a threat as we grow. If captured by a lie early enough, it will be our only truth, and that lie can hinder our growth. As a parent, I know I have a responsibility to feed my infant. If I don't feed him, he will die. However, if I fill his belly with the proper nutrients, he will grow. So, it's safe to say what you feed will grow and what you starve will die. Satan knows this as well. He does not want us to know the truth about who we really are because he knows it nourishes and strengthens us. If we keep eating the lies, we are fed, we will remain weak. Maybe not physically, but spiritually. Food is meant to be fuel for our physical bodies. The types of food we eat will determine our level of strength, vitality, and overall health. The same is true of our mind. If fed the truth of who we are and the true character of God, we'll grow strong knowing we are loved, valued and called. We will destroy Satan's plans and set other captives free.

I was not being fueled by the truth of God's Word and promises. Instead, I was fed lies. What grew in me was the idea that I was worthless and unloved. I was given fuel that kept me malnourished and sick. I became hopeless and depressed, even suicidal. I was not confident and strong in my design.

I felt defeated for a very long time, feeling so alone and rejected. I fed my mind a steady diet of thoughts I'd formed about myself based on the abuse. *You're not worth it. You're a waste of time. You're a reject.*

This tactic of using what others have done to me to define my worth has hands down been the longest lasting battle I have faced. It started when I was an innocent child; young, weak, and impressionable. It led me to believe I had no value or worth for most of my life. It didn't stem from one incident, but Satan took that one moment and forced me to look at it over and over until I viewed everything through the lens of rejection.

As a child, uncertainty was just a way of life. The only thing I ever felt certain of was that my mother would always be my best friend. Although she did her best to encourage me, it wasn't enough to cancel out the negative thoughts and feelings about myself. Mother would encourage me when I colored my Barbie coloring book by pointing out my attention to detail in the way I colored the doll's jewelry and added makeup. She told me I had a beautiful singing voice and gorgeous, high cheekbones. These few precious compliments I remember so well because they were a glimmer of hope in the dark. Even though I didn't believe I was talented or beautiful, her words were like a drop of water in the desert, keeping me going for one more day.

My mother was never one to dole out these compliments regularly. Because they came so few and far between, I cherished them. This wasn't because my mother was an aloof or selfish woman. For her, it was all about living in survival mode as she juggled the cares of a house full of children, endless chores, and an abusive marriage. She worked tirelessly, waking up before her children and falling into bed long after we were tucked in. It took a lot of energy to keep up the standards set before her by the man I called dad. She was to keep an immaculate home, tend to a quarter acre garden, sew clothes, take care of pigs, cows, chickens, rabbits and seven kids. My mother gave of herself in service and did the best she knew how to. She was my hero.

Then suddenly I blinked, and everything changed.

The day after witnessing the abuse, mother took me to her bedroom where we would be alone. Concerned, she asked how many times he raped me and why I hadn't told her. I explained the best I could without getting sick. All at once, all the threats, fear, sadness and confusion came spilling out of me, I felt utterly exposed as I laid out all I had hidden so deep within. The way she looked at me shattered my already fragile heart.

I didn't understand why she looked so angry. I only felt it directed at me. In the silence, I heard my thoughts: *Look at how you disappoint her, see how you messed everything up.*

Mother finally spoke, breaking the long silence to explain that the man I called dad as long as I could remember was not my birth father. Part of me felt relieved, the other part shocked. I sat quietly as she sifted through some papers.

Waves of emotions crashed over me and I could be silent no more. Questions filled my mind and came out of my mouth. What happened to my actual father? Where did he live... could I see him... what did he look like? Where had he been my whole life? Why didn't he want me?

She shared some things about what happened between them when I was a baby. Immaturity and poor decision making were the brunt of the excuse. Mother tried explaining it wasn't my fault, it was just a bad situation... but I never understood completely. I was only twelve and all I could hear was; *you weren't worthy enough for him to stick around. You are worthless. You pitiful, unwanted, waste of time!* The whispering thoughts now became as loud as a freight train.

From the stack of papers she dug out of her closet, she handed me the only picture she had of my father. An 8x10 photo of him at seventeen-years-old, sitting on a bed, smiling. He wore a white button-up shirt, tan pants and sported a long 70s haircut parted straight down the middle. I was drawn to his eyes as I studied his face. We had the very same eyes!

I could feel the sorrow welling up in my little girl heart. How could I feel so excited and so incredibly full of pain at the same time? "Momma, can I talk to him?" I asked, hoping she'd say yes. Unfortunately, she didn't know where he was. This was before the days of Facebook and Google. I wanted to ask more, but I could tell she was done. Once again, silence filled the air as I sat next to her staring into the eyes of my father, wondering and choking back tears.

The words spoken next will be forever etched into my mind…

Mother broke the silence, "I'm sorry about what John did to you, but if anyone ever finds out about what happened last night and it goes to court, I won't stand up and testify for you. I will have to act like I saw nothing. The police would take you from me. For your sake, you shouldn't say anything to anyone." Until that moment, I had not thought about court, police or any of those things. I was only relieved it was over. He was gone and wouldn't return.

After making sure I understood how foolish I would look if I told anyone, I quietly nodded in agreement to stay silent. The conversation was over, but it wasn't over for me! Suddenly, the attack went from bullets to an atomic bomb before I could blink. This bomb took with it all that had been before. It wiped clean the landscape of my life and laid waste to everything I once held on to for hope.

Dazed by those words, I went to my bedroom to process. I needed to go somewhere to stuff what was welling up inside of me. The pain overwhelmed me and threatened to take me out. I wanted to die and a deep sadness settled in to stay for a very long time.

My pain got shoved down into the recesses of my being so that I could function. Early in life I learned that it wasn't okay to talk about feelings. I learned to keep my mouth shut and deal with whatever was thrown my way. I had no voice, and confrontation terrified me. My fear was that if I spoke up, love would be cut off. I wasn't allowed to process things, so I locked my feelings in a closet and tried to ignore the pain.

However, this time was different. As I thought about those words, I could not seem to push them aside and ignore them. I felt more alone than I had ever felt in my entire life. That conversation with my mother validated the lie of rejection. I accepted the lie as truth. In that moment the idea that I was a reject became my reality. I deeply believed I was worthless.

My mother's words had driven this seed of rejection deeper. I wasn't worth standing up for. I was exposed, uncovered, and unprotected, with no one to defend me. My best friend and only safe place had just told me she wouldn't stand up and speak truth on my behalf.

This began a season of heavy darkness. I mourned knowing things would never be the same between my mother and I. Feelings of abandonment and worthlessness settled in to stay as I rehearsed those words, "I'll never stand up for you." They watered the seed of rejection that grew and covered me with deep sorrow.

Then there were the thoughts of my birth father. Every thought was filled with rejection. *Why wasn't he here? Why didn't he find me?* I hated myself for not being enough. Even though mother said it wasn't my fault, there was a little broken girl who felt abandoned and rejected by an earthly father who I was certain would have hated me too.

If I tried to talk to mother about my thoughts and feelings concerning my dad, they were usually dismissed. She would say, "Katy, there's no reason to bring this up anymore. It's done and over. Now leave it alone." *Don't cry, just be strong… tears were for the weak.* If I shed a tear, it was ignored. So I silently screamed at the top of my lungs for help.

I was supposed to be okay, but I wasn't. I wondered what was wrong with me as I watched my mother get on with her life just fine. The abuse had stopped. He was now gone. That part of my life was over... wasn't it?

It was an afternoon like every other. I walked home from the bus stop after school with my siblings, throwing rocks in the creek and breathlessly panting up the mountainous hill that was my driveway. Once I reached the top, there in front of my home was the blue Ford truck.

Terrified, my steps slowed as panic set in. I didn't know what to do. I thought of every possible way of escape as I fought to take each step closer to the front door. My heart was broken.

Why would she let him in? Why is he here? See, she doesn't love you. If she cared about you, he wouldn't be here. You're not worth her protection. What happened to you doesn't even matter to her. You're alone and you always will be. I had walked into an open field completely exposed while the sniper fired from some unseen place. The invisible bullets flew as the attack on my mind ensued.

As I reluctantly entered my home, there was the man I used to call dad, sitting at the kitchen table. Mother was at the stove cooking supper as if nothing ever happened. She didn't even look my way. I slinked off to my room, more wounded than ever, where I quietly cried and waited.

When I could cry no more, I laid in my bed, listening to the crickets outside as the sun began to set. I wished I could float away on that wonderful sound and never come back. The symphony of crickets drowned out my thoughts and swept me away to a peaceful place. I could almost forget where I was when I listened to them.

Just before supper, the voice of my mother jerked me back to the reality that the horrible demon was just on the other side of our three-bedroom trailer. I begged, "Please, I can't live with him. I am scared. What if he tries to touch me again? What if he hurts you?" I said everything I could think of to change her mind, but to no avail.

She told me she was giving him another chance and believed he had changed and would never touch me again. I sat on my bed, utterly confused. *Wait, what just happened? How in the world was this guy a changed man in less than a couple of weeks? What was she thinking?*

I now understand what she was thinking. She had seven kids, no job and had always been a stay-at-home mom. She didn't believe she couldn't provide for us and that he could. My mother wanted to believe he had changed. She bought every lie he fed her blinded by the hope that it was real. Out of desperation she gave him another chance.

Things were calm for a day or so. He was on his best behavior, but I wasn't convinced. I desperately avoided being seen by him. I slept on the couch instead of my bedroom because I thought if he tried to touch me, I would be as close to mother's bedroom as possible. If I needed to scream, she'd hear me. I stayed awake most of the night, scared and determined. If he touched me this time, I would scream no matter what. I'd lay awake listening for the door to open from their bedroom and one night it did.

I heard him coming and tried to act asleep, watching him through squinted eyes. I could see his white t-shirt in the dark coming closer. His heavy body crushed my stomach and legs as he lay on mine. I thought, *Wait, what is he doing? Here? He's going to try to get away with this right in the living room?* I wished I were dead and pretended to be. I held my breath and clenched the blankets close to my neck. The only barrier between us! As soon as he pulled the blanket from my hands, I screamed, "Momma!" It completely took him off guard. He threw the blanket back on me, leaped off of my abdomen and quickly made his way back to his bedroom.

My heart pounded in my chest; hot tears ran down my face. I did it! I finally screamed. I made it stop. I was shocked that it worked! The shock wore off quickly and fear poured over me. Now what?

Right away, I heard yelling coming from my mother's room. Some ugly cursing ensued behind our thin trailer walls. I feared she would get her teeth knocked in for the things she was screaming at him. I didn't know what the banging noises were from. They didn't sound the same as when he would slam her little body into the wall. The door flung open, and he stomped past me with his suitcases in hand. He was gone. I guess that was the banging noises.

I stayed still, curled up in the corner of the couch, as far away from the light as I could get. I was unsure of how she would react. I couldn't bear another disappointed look from her. However, this time, mother came out of her room looking at me with the most regretful eyes. She held me, apologized deeply and swore he would never be back… for real this time.

The next day was a Saturday. My siblings and I were watching cartoons when we heard it, the sound of the blue Ford barreling up the drive. My mother screamed at my older brother to call the cops as she flew out the front door. This 110lb, five foot, three inch woman became a momma bear ready to protect.

Most of the next few minutes were a quick blur of yelling and being passed the responsibility to call the police. My brother was rushing outside to help. There was a lot of yelling and hands flying as she tried to push him back into his truck to leave. He finally got in the cab and drove forward, then suddenly he threw it in reverse and floored it backward, straight into mother. Her tiny frame flew up and into the back of the truck bed. He then kicked it into drive, flinging rocks in the air. He was leaving with her!"

My mind raced, wondering if she was dead, but as he drove off, she jumped up and rolled out of the truck bed. Her entire body landed hard on the ground. She was alive! She was hurt but only with minor injuries! He tore off down the driveway, gravel slinging behind. We never saw him again. My mother had triumphed and had decided, come hell or high water, she was protecting us. She was protecting me...the best way she knew how to.

3

ANGRY GIRL

We soon settled into our new normal. As a single mother with no job, mother did what she could to provide. With the help of local churches and state-funded programs, our basic needs were met, and we were taken care of. We never went without clothes, food or shelter; even if what we wore was secondhand and out of style. I spent a lot of time in welfare lines helping my mother keep the younger children. Even though money was tight, the trade-off was well worth it to have the man I called dad gone for good!

Prior to my mother's freedom from the man who held her captive, I had given little thought to the fact that we were really all she had. With her lack of friendships, my mother needed real adult support during this transition. After being in an abusive relationship for over a decade, she needed healing, guidance, and prayer from women who could lift her up and point her to Jesus. She needed sisters who could take the children in order to give her a moment to breathe, process and just be still.

Mother did eventually make a friend and leaned on her quite a lot. I could often find Paula at our home drinking coffee and listening to mother's woes. She invited mother to go out one night, suggesting she leave the younger children with me. It wasn't unusual for me to help babysit; except I'd never been left alone to do it without mother nearby. It scared me to be up on that wooded mountain at night, in what felt like the middle of nowhere without her. But I wanted to please her. I knew she needed a break, so I put on my best brave face and ensured her I would be fine. Besides, it would only be just this one night. She deserved it and needed a night out.

What began as one night, turned into twice and sometimes three times a week. Her new routine was to leave after dinner with Paula and not return until the middle of the night, long after we had gone to bed. For a while, I didn't know where she was going. I just knew it was frequent. Eventually, I learned she was going to pool halls and bars in a tiny, nearby town. Instead of helping mother through her sorrows, Paula invited her to leave them at the bottom of a bottle. It happened so suddenly. One day she was June Cleaver and the next day she looked like a crazy teenager who had just broken free from an overprotective parent's house. Hearing her come in late, stumbling over furniture through the kitchen on the way to her bedroom, became common. I lay in the living room acting as if I was asleep wondering what happened to my mom and wishing she would come back!

I really believe mother did the best she could for as long as possible. Then one day, she had enough. It was as if overnight she quit being there for us. She still did things for us, but it was different... she was different. Her pain was great, and she found comfort in that intoxicating, clear liquid. A woman I always viewed as a steady pillar of strength slowly crumbled before my eyes. She was overwhelmed with all life had thrown her way and she took it out on us. Not knowing how to deal with her brokenness and pain, she hurt those closest to her.

I've heard it said, "hurting people hurt people". Mother said many hurtful things, but some of the most significant were the threats to leave. When she was at the end of her rope, she'd scream, "If you brats don't shut up and leave me alone, I'm gonna leave you all here to figure it out by yourself."

My youngest sibling was only one-year-old. I knew I couldn't take care of everyone on my own without her. I was terrified she'd follow through and that one day I would come home to find her gone forever. I thought if I tried harder, did more, cleaned better, cared for the children, helped her anyway I could… she would stay. Thankfully she never left us, but I always believed it could happen.

Eventually, she brought home a man to spend the night who would end up staying the next five years. Jim wasn't around for very long when, one day while we were at school, they got married. We found out about the marriage at the dinner table. We had no relationship with him and he didn't seem interested in us. I was glad he wasn't. I didn't trust him, but then, I didn't trust any man.

They went out every weekend and some weeknights. When they weren't out, they drank at home. The mother, who was never without a coffee cup in hand, could now be found with a large plastic cup filled with vodka and Sprite. Although she didn't start drinking first thing in the morning, Jim did, and he drank till his words could no longer be understood. On the occasions he had to stay sober, he was sarcastic and impatient. When he was drunk, this behavior magnified, and his annoying jabs became cutting daggers. My siblings and I were the targets of his verbal abuse.

My friend spent the night with me one evening as she often did to help with the children, so I wasn't home alone as much. Later in the evening, we got hungry, as most 14-year-old teenagers do. Hunting for the perfect late-night snack, we flung open the refrigerator door and there it was, a newly made cheesecake just calling our names! We ate and went to bed with our bellies full.

Later, we were both jolted from our sleep by the sound of Jim bellowing my name from the kitchen. He didn't sound happy. Turning to glance at my clock as I jumped up, I saw it was two in the morning. *What in the world was going on?* I hurried to the kitchen to find out what happened, only to be met with slurred yelling. Apparently, we weren't supposed to touch his cheesecake.

Mother stood behind him while he yelled and called me names. Fat Pig. Stupid loud-mouth girl. Selfish slob. She never stopped him. She didn't say a word. Angry, hurt and embarrassed, I cried, "Momma! Please!? Say something! Make him stop!" Before she could respond, with a finger wagging in my face, Jim screamed, "You and your stupid friend ate all my cheesecake and I'm tired of you doing whatever you want to around here."

As he held out an almost empty pie plate, I couldn't believe my eyes. "Jim, we only ate two pieces. I don't know what happened to the rest!" My sentence barely came out of my mouth before Jim screamed, "Shut your mouth and get out of my face you little liar."

I'm certain I've carried a little bag of anger with me since I could remember. I picked up new events to add to it along the way until it became too heavy to carry. This heavy anger overflowed its bag, spilling into a new larger one I'd picked up to hold resentment. My bag of resentment filled quickly, and so I held yet another. This bag carried hate.

I resented mother for not protecting me. For marrying Jim without even asking how I felt about it. I resented her for changing, hating that she drank. I hated being alone. I hated she wouldn't stand up for me. I hated Jim. I hated that my real dad wasn't there to rescue me from it all. I hated just about everything and everyone, including myself. The weight of all those bags was immense, and I was tired of carrying them. However, it seemed they were a part of me now. They were so intertwined with my existence that they could not be removed.

I thought about killing myself often to stop the pain. As my head lay on the pillow each night, I'd beg my body not to wake up. Drifting off to sleep, I'd hear the whispering thoughts. *You don't matter. You'll never be good enough. No one loves you. You're all alone... why don't you just die, and all this will be over.* The enemy was working to defeat me with every weapon in his arsenal. The mind is his favorite battleground, because it's where our thoughts give birth to actions. If he could completely convince me life wasn't worth living, maybe I would take myself out before I became a greater threat.

The influential thoughts falsely reminded me I was rejected, unloved, ugly, and worthless. These thoughts were an attempt to create a reality that life was hopeless. If I believed the words in my mind, then maybe I would act on them, ultimately leading to my demise. As a child, I wasn't aware that Satan could influence my thoughts in an attempt to provoke a reaction (John 13:2). He whispers lies and looks for any opportunity to deceive us (John 8:44). When given the opportunity, Satan is ready to remind us of the labels we believe about ourselves. He will point out reasons why we should believe them as truth. He whispers, "See? You always mess everything up. You are worthless. No one loves you." It sounds like us when we hear the accusations and lies, but it is not.

What happened to me was very real. It was hard and painful. It was painful to have been a victim of sexual abuse and difficult to live with the messages it sent about my worth. It was painful to lose the relationship I had with my mother. It was challenging to see the pedestal I'd placed her on come crashing down. It was painful to feel abandoned. The pain was great; the responsibility was heavy and the anger seething below the surface was scary. Because of these events, I believed a lie about who I was.

It was hard to figure out how to deal with all I was feeling on my own. I had no positive input or anyone to encourage me. I did not know how to encourage myself! Truth wasn't presented to cancel out the lies. I didn't even know I was being lied to. Because of the sexual abuse, I already believed that I was unloved and worthless. The enemy used these lies as foundational beliefs to shape the view I had of myself and the world around me. When my mother took a huge step back, it wounded my heart, and I saw it as a personal jab at my value. I wasn't "worth" her time. The enemy of my soul suggested these thoughts and I grabbed ahold of them hook, line and sinker. I was convinced that what I thought about myself was true.

At fourteen, I began to cut myself in an attempt to release the pain. This went on for months. As I bled, I imagined my emotional pain being released from my physical pain. I kept cutting, but the pain in my heart remained. Sitting on my bedroom floor, I watched as the blood ran down my ankle. I contemplated ending my life and finally decided enough was enough. I slit my wrists and went to sleep, hoping never to wake. Fortunately for me, I cut the wrong way. When I awoke, I heard a whisper, "See, you dumb girl! You can't even do that right."

My desire wasn't to die, but I didn't want to live my current life anymore. I was drowning in despair with no one to throw me a life preserver. I was unaware that Jesus was my life preserver. When the waves crashed all around and threatened to drown me with each hit, He was always there to pull me right back up to the surface. The enemy wanted me dead. I'm so thankful God had another plan!

4

THERE HAS TO BE ANOTHER WAY

By the age of fifteen, I was desperate to get out of my home. I began making some hard choices. I look back on these choices now and wonder how things would have been different if someone had stepped into my life as a voice of reason. What would have happened if just one person would have recognized my pain and desperation and invested time and love into me?

If someone had been speaking truth into my life, discipling me and saying no when I needed to hear no, I believe I would have been spared years of pain. This is one reason I am drawn to teens. I want to be that voice that speaks truth and points them to God. We never know how just one ten-minute conversation can affect another's life. We can let them know they are loved, seen, and cared for. It's worth the time!

I've since learned, no matter how many times teenagers say they don't need help, they still need loving guidance and training. I believe it's good to leave room for mistakes to be made on their own. This is how we learn. But we don't just watch a toddler walk to the top of the stairs and think, *well, they'll learn the hard way.* No, we grab a hand and help them take each step. This is what I so desperately needed.

As a high school freshman, I cared about all the things relevant to girls my age; hair, make-up, clothes and who to go to spring formal with. I had friends who kept me sane with silly antics and cry fests when I needed them. I also had those close few that were more like family and whose mothers even treated me like their own. This didn't mean they gave me guidance, but at least they showed me love. None of them were aware of the ugly undercurrent of pain flowing through me. If they were, they didn't know what to say.

However, while most girls my age were planning what they would do for the weekend, I was planning my quickest escape route from the life I lived. I counted down the days until I would be free. I couldn't stand the thought of staying one day past my eighteenth birthday. My plan was to be packed the week before and to run as far away from Jim as I could. I was okay in the meantime, as long as I had my friends and their families to distract me.

On an afternoon like any other, I got off the bus and walked home with my siblings and into the house to get ready for chores and homework. Jim, who had no job, was usually home when we arrived. He'd either be watching T.V. with a beer in hand or passed out in bed. However, this afternoon he was sitting at the kitchen table with my mother, waiting for us to arrive. Motioning for us to gather around the wooden farm style table, Jim announced he'd finally found a job, and we were moving to Kentucky. Oh, and we are leaving next week.

I panicked. The few close friends that I had made my life bearable. I couldn't be alone again... I wouldn't. I cried and contemplated through most of the night until an idea came to me! I would ask one of my closest friends, Lindsey, to let me move in with her! It was so crazy that I honestly didn't think it would work, but I was desperate. I knew I'd have to open up and explain a little more about why I was asking. The next day, I shared with my friend and then her family. They didn't need many details before it was a resounding, YES! I was welcome to stay with them as long as I liked.

As soon as I had an answer, I went to my mother to plead my case. I couldn't imagine her saying yes to losing her free babysitter, but I had to try. To my surprise, she agreed with one stipulation; that I come home during the summer. I could hardly believe how easy it was! I was so relieved that I wouldn't have to wait until I was eighteen to get away from Jim.

This was not a rebellious act to run wild as a teen. Rather, I saw it as a glimmer of hope for peace and some sort of stability. I had no problem with having responsibilities and being told what to do. What I had a problem with was living with the fear of messing up and getting a verbal lashing. I was tired of being cursed at and called names that cut me deeply. I had a problem with being locked out of my home with my siblings being unable to use the bathroom so Jim could watch TV. I hated being responsible for the well-being and safety of my siblings so often. Even if I wasn't asked, they expected me to care for them. Being a people pleaser and rule follower, I wanted to help and wanted to do it right. I just couldn't handle the weight of it all. I felt as though what I did was never enough.

It elated me to be under the authority of Dan and Mary. They would watch out for my well-being. I was so grateful to them for allowing me to come that I never wanted to ask for anything. Thankfully, I didn't have to. They anticipated my basic needs and considered me. They didn't have a lot, but they shared what they had and treated me with so much kindness. Lindsey's house was a place where I felt safe and free to just be a kid.

Their family was noticeably different. Mary cooked pancakes with chocolate chips in them. She made sandwiches for school and made sure we all wore our seatbelts when we left. She asked everyone about their day and took time to listen. I noticed the closeness and connection they had with one another. I noted how Dan, Mary and all three of the children cared for their grandparents who lived next door, checking on them often and taking time to chat.

Dan and Mary loved each other openly with hugs and kisses before leaving the house, when returning home, and before bed. Mean or harsh words never came out of their mouths. They seemed to be the best of friends. Problems were talked through openly without screaming at one another. They discussed challenges their children faced and made it a family affair. It was unlike anything I'd ever experienced. I soaked up every ounce like a sponge.

The cutting stopped as I felt hopeful for the future. Mary invited me to stay until I graduated high school if I wanted to. I did a little happy dance on the inside! Stay? Of course, I wanted to! I never wanted to leave. It meant so much to feel seen and wanted. I was so grateful to have them in my life. They gave love, time and money without ever asking for anything in return.

I wasn't used to having something done for me without the guilt that I owed a debt. Lindsey's family demonstrated what it felt like to receive, with no strings attached. I still battled feeling as though I didn't deserve kindness because I believed I wasn't worth it. Mary reminded me with her famous words, "Just say thank you and go on."

That summer, Lindsey's parents drove me to Kentucky. I was both excited and nervous to be home with my family. I missed my siblings and mother. I didn't miss Jim and his jeering remarks. Reminding myself it would only be for the summer kept me hopeful. Soon after I arrived and settled in, I realized the only thing that had changed was the location.

Jim had acquired a tiny two-bedroom trailer home to house all six of the remaining children. With two adults, plus me, living quarters were tight, to say the least. Jim and mother made friends in the trailer park, and they spent much of the time at their place. If they weren't with them, they were locked in their bedroom with the smell of marijuana pouring out into the living room nearby. I was ready to run! I wanted to go back to Lindsey's, take my siblings with me, and be done with this crazy life. I felt bad for them, but I couldn't stay.

I spent a lot of time outside watching my siblings play in the yard. On a hot June afternoon, I was sitting in a lawn chair watching my brother, Matt, ride his tricycle in the front yard. I noticed a tall boy about my age as he walked up the road with jeans that were too big for him and sagging off his waist. I had noticed him before. He walked by my house a few times a day. He was shy, always looking at the ground or quickly glancing my way and back down, but he never spoke.

Matt was feeling extra friendly this particular afternoon and as the boy walked by, he shouted, "Hi! I'm Matt! What's your name?" Stopping, he spoke to Matt and then introduced himself to me. His name was Ron. He was seventeen and just a little older than I was. He only lived a few houses down. Soon, we began finding every reason to hang out. A boy had never shown me the kind of attention he did. It didn't take long before I was enamored. He was a welcome distraction to help pass the time.

I was so desperate for love and attention, and Ron gave it to me. Unfortunately, I felt I needed to perform to keep it, so I gave myself away. I didn't value myself or my sexuality. No one else had. Why should I? I reasoned that my innocence had already been stolen, so why should I care? What value was there in saving myself? I believed I was damaged goods; a factory defect who wasn't worth paying full price for.

I spent most of the few weeks I had left before going back to Lindsey's, intoxicated with puppy love and drugs. I was desperate to get away from my reality. Ron appeared he didn't have a care in the world. Maybe marijuana was my answer too? I wanted the carefree, chill attitude that he carried.

Mother was so distracted with her life that she never noticed when I was high. If she knew, she never mentioned it. I wish she would have! On the inside, I was crying out for someone to say, "Hey this is not good for you. You know it and I know it. Put it down, walk away, end this relationship." I wanted to hear the word, "NO." I wanted to hear, "I care about you and don't want you to ruin your life." Instead, I heard silence.

I am so thankful God never stopped whispering, "This way." Even when I took the wrong path, he put up detour signs and exit ramps everywhere! I was being cared for far more than I ever knew. He never stopped protecting me, even when I felt unprotected. No matter how alone I felt, He was always right there with me.

With summer winding down, it was time to leave it all behind. Ron didn't take the news well and, in a desperate attempt to get me to stay, proposed on his front porch. Not exactly romantic, but it was sweet. As a fifteen-year-old, I wasn't quite ready for that. We hadn't known each other long enough for the type of commitment he was asking of me. I promised we would talk every day, but I had to go for now. As much as I enjoyed his attention, it wasn't enough to stay. My new life was calling!

A week before sophomore year started, I made plans to go back. "What's a good day for Lindsey's parents to come get me for school?" I asked Mother. Her reply was not what I expected. "Jim and I have decided you should stay here. We need you." I felt sick to my stomach and anguish swept over me. *No! How could she? I can't stay,* I thought frantically.

I'd pushed back the sadness as it tried to overwhelm me all summer by holding onto the hope of leaving. There was a light at the end of the tunnel and now that light had a big rockslide of boulders covering it. I was blocked and trapped in the darkness. I had experienced a life, even for a short time, with Lindsey's family that I didn't want to live without.

I knew why they wanted me to stay. They didn't want to lose their babysitter because Jim didn't enjoy having to share my mother's attention with the children. My presence freed up more of her time. He fought as hard to keep me from leaving as I fought to go. It wasn't because he loved me that he wanted me to stay. It wasn't even in him to act as though he liked me. He only spoke rude words to me. According to Jim, my name wasn't Katy, it was "little snot." If he felt particularly feisty, it was "little b***h" which was usually followed by jabs about my weight, hair or clothes. No, he didn't want me to stay home because he cared about me.

I gave every possible argument for why I had to go back and eventually I was allowed to leave. However, a couple of months after school started, I received a phone call from mother. It was strange because she didn't normally call. After establishing how everyone was doing, she got straight to the point. I was to be on the next Greyhound bus home.

Devastated, I did as I was told. Sadness settled on me like a wet, heavy blanket. I hated going back to Jim's verbal abuse and I couldn't stand watching alcohol steal my mother right before my eyes. I wasn't home long before I knew I had to find a way to get back out, even if it meant running away.

Desperation made me willing to do anything. Desperation causes us to make very rash decisions. It can blind us and cloud our judgment. When I reunited with Ron, we talked a lot about running away from it all together. Ron was living with his sister, a thousand miles away from home, because his mom didn't want to deal with him anymore. Something about a robbery and drugs. There were red flags everywhere, but I didn't see them!

Ron's sister, Becky, knew about the spontaneous proposal before I left and told me that if we were married, I could be emancipated. That meant I could be free! He was almost eighteen, and I was only months away from being sixteen. We could do this! Marriage sounded like a pretty good idea. However, I didn't understand the sanctity of it. I was fifteen and desperate; marriage was only a means to an end.

Mother would have to agree to sign the papers, allowing the marriage, which I was certain she'd refuse. When I presented her with the idea, astonishingly, with little resistance, she agreed. The same woman, who just months before was determined I come home, was now ready to sign me away to this young man she didn't even know. Come to think of it, a young man I didn't really know, either.

I will never understand what caused her to say yes. Maybe she felt tired or thought I would find a way to leave, anyway. She knew I was miserable. The anger and frustration I kept pent up for so long started spewing out of me. I finally stopped caring about rocking the boat and worrying about the consequences. I went on strike at home, refusing to babysit any longer. I was no longer the rule following, compliant 'yes' girl. I did normal chores and school, but that was it. I figured anything she did to me couldn't compare to what I had already been through. I had nothing left to lose, so why keep trying?

Two months before my sixteenth birthday, Ron and I married. We rented a tiny trailer for forty dollars a week with a hole in the hallway floor we had to jump across to get to the back bedroom. We had no car and little money, but I didn't care. I was willing to work as hard as I needed to make it on my own. I was desperate and determined I would never go back home. I was also determined to graduate from high school. With two years left to go, graduating seemed an impossible task. I set up a meeting to speak with the guidance counselor about my situation.

The loud speaker crackled, "Mrs. Smith, Please send Katy to the office." I quickly gathered up my things while ignoring all the comments from my classmates, who were still acting like children. I didn't have time for that anymore. I felt like an adult now. It was time to act like one. I had never been in trouble at school a day in my life. I prided myself on being the "good girl" and performing at a standard that adults would be pleased with. I also liked flying under the radar with as little attention as necessary. I did what I was supposed to, hoping I wouldn't be noticed. If I was doing something I shouldn't, it certainly wouldn't have been at school. No, I wasn't being summoned because I had pulled the fire alarm or been caught cheating on a test.

Pushing the counselor's heavy brown door open, a gray-haired woman with a friendly face greeted me. "Come on in here sweetie!" she said with a thick southern draw as she motioned to the nearby chair, "Have you a seat right here!"

Mrs. Gray explained how she already knew about my situation and wanted to help me accomplish my goal to graduate. "I see here from your transcripts you have thirty-one credits and your grades are good. That's more than you need to graduate from this school."

My stomach wrenched. I was nervous and excited about this news. My mind was reeling as I wondered what this could mean for me. She continued, "It looks like all you need to graduate after your junior year, per the state's requirements, would be an English four class. We offer a night class to accelerated students that you can take right here at the school. If you pass it, along with all your other classes, you could graduate as a junior. Would you like to do that?"

My heart was beating wildly! "Yes, I would be more than happy to do that!" I blurted out. What a gift, I thought. I must be the luckiest girl. I now know that luck had nothing to do with it. I didn't recognize it then, but the favor of God was resting on me long before I understood what favor was. I was certain I could work part time and finish school now!

It didn't take long to find a job. I began working as a waitress at a local restaurant. Ron worked as a painter's assistant with his brother-in-law. Between the two of us, we made enough to cover basic living expenses and our bad habits with a little left over for food. As long as the bills were paid, I didn't care. I viewed life through a very narrow lens. A lens that saw no plans or hope for a future, only to survive today. Whatever the cost and whatever the compromise.

Our trailer was barely furnished, but I really didn't mind. I was grateful for what I had. We slept on a donated, queen water bed mattress without a frame. One evening, Ron woke in the middle of the night to use the bathroom and smoke. It's pretty difficult to stay asleep on a waterbed mattress when someone is moving. Especially one that required crawling on hands and knees to get out of. I felt him crawling back in the bed as he gathered the ashtray and lighter. He began to breathe deeply and exhale slowly as I drifted back to sleep.

Suddenly, I jolted awake, and I immediately noticed the orange glow that lit the darkness. I rolled over toward the light and was greeted by flames inches from my head. Fumbling to get out of the waterbed, I screamed to wake Ron up. We both ran around, grabbing anything we could use to extinguish the flames. We quickly soaked the floor with bowls of water. It didn't take long before all that remained was a hole in the carpet, exposing the thin wood beneath.

Falling asleep with a cigarette in his hand wasn't an isolated incident for Ron. There were many irresponsible things that I overlooked and engaged in that put my life in danger. I could hear the warning sirens faintly in the distance getting louder and louder, yet I continued to ignore them. The phone was ringing off the hook with my wake-up call. I had to answer! This had to stop!

It was at that moment when I realized how bad it could have been and how the decisions of those around me truly affected my life. I agreed to join Ron in smoking pot, but soon he needed more. This was where I began to draw the line for myself. It scared me to partake in the types of drugs Ron was getting involved with. Soon, I would stay home while he went to various places to hang out. To say I was uncomfortable in the environments he was going into was an understatement.

Because I cared about him, I tried changing his mind. I pled my case while explaining all my worries and concerns for his well-being. When I brought it up, he would get angry and throw things around our little trailer, at the walls, and at me. He was changing, but his mind was not.

Eventually, I discovered he was selling drugs. It then became clear how we had money for our own drugs and alcohol. Soon after discovering this truth, I uncovered where he was spending most of his time. He had a girlfriend in our trailer park that was more accepting of his lifestyle. What did I get myself into?

After nine months, I decided I couldn't take one more day. Something inside of me wouldn't stand for it anymore. *What am I going to do? I can't go back and live with mother, but I can't just sit here like this.*

Feeling overwhelmed and helpless, I called the only other person I knew that might help, Ron's sister, Becky. After explaining what I'd learned, she suggested I come stay with her for a while, hoping Ron would get his act together. In my sixteen-year-old mind, I pictured the results of my actions. I would leave and Ron would soon beg me to come back, telling me I was the most important thing in the world to him. Somehow, he would realize that I was worth changing his lifestyle for. He would stop using drugs and cheating on me. However, this was not the way the story would go.

The opposite happened. When I left, Ron left. He got on a bus and went thousands of miles back to his home deep in the south, never to be seen again. My heart broke in a new way. My love for him was greater than I could describe. The idea of life without him was unbearable. The heartbreak was heavy, but the feeling of abandonment was overwhelming. *He didn't even try? What was so unlovable about me? Why wasn't I worth it?*

Being exhausted and wobbly after that battle left me in the perfect position for the enemy to take his shot. This battle was one that he hoped would leave me knocked out for good! I heard the whisper, *you're not enough, you're trash, no one loves you… you don't matter.* These beliefs grew deep roots in my heart and took over my thoughts. Without warning, the hedge grew thicker, trapping me yet again behind enemy lies.

5

LET ME PUT THESE BLINDERS ON

I left my home behind to move in with Becky and her husband, Troy. When Ron left, I couldn't afford to keep it and go to school. Besides, Becky was certain it wasn't suitable or safe. I would stay with them until I could afford to buy a car and then find a place to rent on my own. It was painfully clear that I couldn't do that with the income from the small-town diner. After graduation, Becky recommended I get a job with her.

We now worked and lived full time together. It didn't take long before the tension began mounting between us. Becky grouped people into two categories: people she tolerated and people she targeted. If she ever locked her target on someone, they would not escape her wrath. My goal was to stay in the "tolerated" group as long as possible because I witnessed what it looked like to be on her bad side. If you ever ticked her off, she would be sure you regretted the day you met her. She was slowly shoving me across the line from tolerated to targeted and I didn't know why. So, I kept my head down, my mouth shut, and tried to stay out of the way.

I wasn't sure what to expect each day with her. One moment she would be happy and smiling about everything and the next moment she would erupt in anger over the smallest thing. The tone of her snide remarks made me want to stay as far away from her as possible, fearing she'd swing at any moment. She was incredibly jealous and very often accused her husband of flirting with other women. Then one day, out of nowhere, I overheard her accuse him of flirting with me! There was no reason for the accusation, yet she said it.

Troy and I didn't speak outside of formalities, and we were never alone. In my eyes, he was an old man. He was nice, but I didn't trust any older men and never felt comfortable being left alone with him. If she left and he was home, I went for a walk or played outside with their children, who were four and seven. They were old enough to tell if I did something I shouldn't have. She had no reason to worry about me, but she didn't know of my past abuse. She didn't know I was extra cautious not to entice unwanted attention from any man. At least now I understood why she'd started treating me differently.

It was hard being somewhere I knew I wasn't wanted. Becky was ready for me to go and I was about to walk right into the very reason she needed to tip the scale. One evening, I barreled into the bathroom, focused on trying not to wet my pants. Unfortunately for me, Becky was taking a bath and forgot to lock the door. As I flung the door open, she shrieked, "Get out!" Red faced, I quickly shut the door.

Have you ever wished you could hit rewind on a moment, go back and do it right? Boy, did I wish I had a remote-control for that one. Within minutes, the bathroom door flung back open with Becky in her towel screaming at me to get out of her house! Her reaction felt like a sledgehammer blow to the gut. I packed my bags and became homeless at seventeen.

I walked to the closest shelter I could find, a baseball dug-out. As I laid down and looked up at the stars, I wondered how I got here and if God was even real. I was certain that if He were real; He didn't care about me. I'd heard that God was good, and that He cared about His children. I knew I was His child, but how could a good God let His child be mercilessly abused? How could a good God leave me alone with no way out? Why hadn't He rescued me? An overwhelming sadness came over me as I pondered my insignificance and sleep eluded me.

When daylight broke, I walked to the nearest payphone to call my boss, Jerry, and explain why I wouldn't be in for my shift. After sharing the highlights of the previous day, without hesitation, he asked if he could give me a ride to work. I was so relieved to be able to work, but I knew I wouldn't be safe sleeping on the streets of that city. I was hesitant to accept his offer to pick me up, but I felt it was my only choice. What came next was even more surprising. He said, "Oh, and, hey. If you need a place to stay, I have an extra room. You're welcome to it."

Red lights were flashing in my mind, sirens blaring in my ear—I knew immediately that it was a bad idea. Jerry was much older than me, with two small children and a live-in girlfriend. For a split second, I wondered how she would feel about me being there.

Wisdom would have won here if given the chance. However, at that moment, I was desperate to keep my job and not have to go back to my mother's or sleep outside again. My response was quick. "Yes, if you're sure. That would be great." Even though I felt uncertain about my decision, I figured it would only be for a short time until I could gather my finances.

While I waited for Jerry to arrive, I pondered how this was all going to work. I was nervous and sick to my stomach, but I pushed those feelings aside while reminding myself I needed a place to stay. I knew I would be at the mercy of a man I barely knew. I wanted to believe he would be safe. I told myself he was good. Ignoring all the warning sirens going off in my mind, I fearfully plowed forward. Alone, wounded, and scared, I was available prey for the predator.

Maybe as you read this you're thinking, "Girl!? You're crazy! Go home!" That's what I said to myself the minute I walked into his house. Looking back at the results of this decision, I can clearly see what fear once made blurry. I didn't want to see the consequences of my decisions. I ignored every voice of reason, drowning it out with excuses. This one desperate decision caused me years of great pain and heartache. This would be the beginning of a long period of darkness, like I had never known.

As I arrived, the house seemed to have been ransacked. All signs that children were in the home were removed; no beds or toys were left. Jerry's girlfriend had cleaned out all her things, too. Only remnants scattered on the floors. I gave myself a little pep talk to keep from running out the door I had just walked through. *Don't worry about it, you won't be here long. Just put your things down and breathe. Stay calm. You only need this for a short time. I'm sure there is an explanation for all of this.*

After sitting my things down, I nervously asked what happened. Every question was met nonchalantly. His careless attitude about losing his family was concerning. From what I gathered, his girlfriend had been cheating on him and he went to jail for domestic assault. He told me it was her fault, though. Because she was outside yelling for the neighbors to call the cops, he drug her back inside. Since she was apparently crazy, he had to hold her down on the ground and cover her mouth to get her to stop screaming, which left bruises on her. He was fully convinced it was only because the police had to take someone to jail when they're called for domestic violence that he went. Not because he'd done anything wrong. By the time he got out of jail the next day, she'd taken all her things along with the children and left. He assured me it was "no big deal" and was glad she was gone.

Even though it sounded like quite a big deal, I shrugged it off and excused it away. What did I know? I wasn't there. I just needed a place for a little while. Sure, the red flags were everywhere, but I just couldn't see them. I was intentionally colorblind. If I paid attention to the warnings, I would have to leave, but where could I go?

There are moments in our lives when we realize we have made a poor decision that's gotten us off track. This is typically the time to evaluate and course correct. I had this realization many times during those first couple of months of living with Jerry. Nevertheless, I charged ahead with sheer determination. If I had listened to the voice of reason, I would've ran as fast as I could, right back home, and figured out a different way. But I didn't. I refused to acknowledge it even though I heard that voice shouting, "STOP! TURN AROUND! DEAD END, RUN!"

The first few weeks in my new place were relatively uneventful, aside from a few comments from co-workers about sleeping with the boss. I shrugged them off, knowing I had no intention of that. I was beginning to wonder if Jerry was making our arrangement out to be more than it was. He was overly kind in those first weeks and refused to let me pay rent, or anything, for that matter.

Since I didn't have a vehicle, I rode to and from work with him. After long shifts, we'd go out to breakfast together, and he insisted on paying the bill. He set up outings and took me to see places I'd never been. After overhearing a phone conversation with my best friend, who I really missed, he offered to drive me over three hours to see her.

The only problem was that I sensed an unspoken expectation rising. I was racking up an invisible "you own me" list. I knew it couldn't go on this way, and it soon became apparent that Jerry had ideas about how I could pay him back. When the time came for the expected payment, I did not know how to say no. I fell, hook, line and sinker, into a trap.

After tremendous pressure, I submitted to his continued requests. I worried that if I kept resisting, he'd kick me out. Suddenly, I felt as though I owed him and now I needed him to survive. Somehow, I found myself tangled in a web of bad decisions and regret. Every time I thought things were out of hand and I should leave, I imagined all the reasons I couldn't. I reluctantly entered into a very controlling relationship with a man who exploited my misfortune for his gain. Jerry would later use this very moment as a weapon. Saying yes to him was the ammunition he needed to remind me of the pitiful state I was in before he rescued me. The instant I traded my body for provision, I traded any hope of being treated with dignity.

This mindset didn't occur all at once. It was a slow and subtle process of compromising what I felt was right for what I feared I must do. Each decision I made pulled me further from a path of freedom and independence and directed me to one of bondage and slavery. I didn't decide to be a slave by saying, "Oh, I think this looks like a good idea." Rather, I found myself distracted by things that seemed good until I looked up and found I had willingly walked into an invisible, self-imposed prison.

Once I stepped inside and heard the door shut, I looked up and realized everything looked very different. Standing alone in that cell, I was dazed and wondered what had happened and how did I get here? I heard the whisper in my mind, you're stuck now. You'll never leave. Each time I heard that lie, I'd run to the prison door and frantically shake the bars with all intentions of getting free. I'd scream, "NO I won't stay here." But as soon as my hand touched the doorknob, the prison guard named Fear would show up and stand in my path, reminding me of all the reasons I needed to shut up and sit down.

There is a trick that circuses once used to keep their elephants from running away. Baby elephants were trained by tying the end of a rope around their leg to a stake in the ground. Because the elephants are small, only a thin rope is required. At first, they'll struggle and pull, but eventually they realize they can't break free and it hurts to try. They will stop pulling and give up, resigned to their captivity. Before long, those cute babies grow into massive creatures with immense strength. This same thin rope is all that's needed to keep them secured. They think the rope can still hold them and they never try to break free.

I, too, felt like that baby elephant all grown up. Eventually, I believed the lie that I was now captive and didn't fight. Even though the door was left completely unlocked, I believed I was trapped.

It didn't take long to find out why his ex-girlfriend had left. I should've listened to the voice in my head that screamed "Run!" when he explained how it was her fault he went to jail for domestic assault. I was never sure which version of Jerry I would get or what new behavior I'd learn about that day. One moment he'd treat me with kindness, and the next moment I was one step above a garbage can.

Once I became the live-in girlfriend, I also became his property. He made sure I knew he was the boss, both at work and at home. He frequently reminded me how desolate I'd be without him. I was sure he was right, and I detested him for it. I hated myself even more.

Why did I say yes!? What's wrong with me?! Just as I did when I was a little girl, I dreamed about being brave enough to leave. I'd imagine him coming home from work and I would be gone. At work, when he degraded me in front of my co-workers, I imagined myself ripping off my uniform and walking straight out the door. Envisioning myself proudly marching down the road, to the red light, then... no wait. Then where? Walk out to where?! Never mind, what was I thinking?

I'd swam too far into stormy waters and got stuck. The undercurrent pulled me further and further from shore without a rescue boat in sight. After fighting to stay afloat for so long, I was mentally and emotionally exhausted. Believing this was it for me, I gave up and let the current take me wherever it wanted to go.

I endured public ridicule and shaming at my job. Jerry liked to call me terrible names in front of the other staff. He would tell me to shut up frequently in order to remind me who was in charge. Occasionally, following a verbal assault at work, I'd speak up for myself in front of the others. I paid for it later. I was ignored and given the silent treatment for days. This type of punishment only validated the belief that I was unimportant and not worth much, if anything at all.

Jerry believed women were put on earth for his pleasure. Our shifts together were difficult for me to endure for this very reason. I stood by as I watched him ogle women and listened as he made degrading comments about them. It was hard to ignore. He was loud and proud of his opinion. I was so embarrassed as my co-workers looked on with their sympathetic eyes. I'm sure they wondered, "Aren't you going to say something?"

Of course, I wanted to say something. I wanted to say a lot of something. But I knew to keep my mouth shut. In the past, when I confronted Jerry about the way those types of things made me feel, it always ended the same. I would speak up and he responded with scary rage, throwing demeaning word daggers that hurt deeply. I dared not continue to make my appeal. The wounds from those encounters left me weak and wondering if he was right, that it was my fault.

He was great at making me feel as though I did something wrong all the time. If I didn't relent during the first round, he'd pull out the big guns. "If you don't shut up right now, you're going to be out on the street where I found you." The reminder of my lowest point and how he "rescued" me was his way of staying in control. It was his power and his words that defeated me every time. "If it weren't for me, you'd be out on the street somewhere."

The times I remained stubborn and kept trying to get him to see how my heart was broken over his behavior, his response was a devastating blow. "If you don't like it, then leave." Those words caused me more pain than the name calling. I knew those words were exactly what I needed to do. It was as if there was an invisible magnetic pull I couldn't break free from. So, I stayed frozen, stuck in a life I didn't want to be in.

6

THE LAND OF NEVER ENOUGH

For two more years, things stayed the same. He hurled abuse, and I stayed. When I was nineteen, we found out we were expecting a son. I resolved to stay with sheer determination and fight with every stubborn bone in my body to avoid the thing I feared more than anything: being a single mom. This was out of the question because I was certain it would be impossible. I only had a minimum wage job and, wait… even that was being taken. At four months pregnant, he took me off the schedule. He was my boss, and I had to obey. "You don't need to work. I take care of you and besides, women should be at home doing dishes, barefoot and pregnant," he laughed. *Oh, great! That's what he thinks? Wonderful!*

Still, I had no choice, or so I thought. I was held captive by the belief that I couldn't make it without him now. After two years, I still had no vehicle and relied on him for everything. I was painfully unaware that God could and would take care of me if I let Him. By now, I'd been let out of my cell and could freely roam the prison camp of my mind. However, I dared not venture far. I kept my eyes on the rocky ground, never looking up to see that freedom was just on the other side and I could walk right out!

If I looked up with the hope that I could see a glimpse of what could be, the lies were the lens I viewed life through. Instead of seeing the truth of what my life could be like if I chose freedom, I saw fear, despair, depression, and hopelessness. These lies held up their warnings and reminders of my worthlessness, mistakes, and inadequacy.

Unfortunately, I didn't know God yet. Sure, I'd heard of Him but I was unaware of who He really was. When I was a tween, my heart melted for Leonardo DiCaprio. I bought every *Seventeen* magazine with his picture in it I could afford and tried to keep up with his life. The magazine interviews gave me information about Leo; his favorite color, what his dog's name was and if he was dating anyone. I always held my breath before reading the answer to that last question. Even with all the information I could gather about him, I still didn't know Leonardo DiCaprio. I only knew of him. I wasn't in close relationship with him. Let's state the obvious. I wasn't even in his circle of acquaintances. I couldn't possibly know his character, his ticks, what makes him mad, what makes him laugh, what drove him to do what he did. The same was true for God, except I hadn't even read up on Him. I only knew what I had been told. My view of God was distorted, small, and very wrong.

Growing up, I often heard mother say, "We can't afford that." I wore hand-me-downs, and we survived thanks to government assistance. Most of the things we owned were donated. We drove an old, decommissioned, rusty church van that had been given to us. It was clear, from the rusty hole in the driver's side floor board and ripped seat covers, why it was no longer in use. We frequented food pantry lines and ate out-of-date food items. While my friends had Fruit Loops with regular milk, we ate off-brand bran-puffs with powdered milk. Even though our basic needs were met, I felt the lack. Growing up like this left me living in the land of Never-Enough, with the idea that "you better take all you can while you can."

A poverty mindset caused me to believe the lie that God was not a good provider. Even worse, I believed He didn't care about my needs at all. I was unaware that God was a God of abundance, and not only could he take care of me, but He would!

I believed the lie that it was all up to me to get what I needed in this life. The phrase "If it is to be, it's up to me," scared me to death. If it was up to me, I wouldn't have anything. I believed I was a helpless victim with no power or control. I lived as a leaf blown onto a rushing river going where the water takes it. I was merely along for the ride. I believed everything that happened to me resulted from an outside force, one to which I had no control. For so long, I thought I had to deal with whatever came at me as my "lot in life". I never thought I had the option to turn and fight the current.

I lived with a crippling fear that I wouldn't have what I needed or would be homeless again. Even though it was hard, living with Jerry provided me a nice home and good food. I had as much as I wanted and more than I needed. This was all it took to convince me to stay. I never wanted to go back to the land of Never-Enough.

Once our son was born, I expected Jerry would want to be involved more at home. Somehow, we would become a family and he'd value me as the mother of his child.

A week after the arrival of our firstborn, my dreams came crashing down. All the beautifully painted pictures I had imagined were blown away by a spin up tornado. I hate tornadoes!

Two weeks after bringing our newborn home, his boss announced that Jerry would be leaving for Wisconsin.

"Doesn't he know you just had a baby?" I asked, frustrated with this news. "You haven't even had time to be home with us!"

"Yes, Kathryn, he knows!" Jerry replied with a huff as he walked into the other room. I followed, "Okay. Do you have to go? Can't he send someone else?"

"I'm going Kathryn, I already told him I would."

He liked to call me by my full name when he was being firm and would not change his mind. "I want to go. He asked me over everyone else! It is a great opportunity. I could make that store great!" He replied while packing his suitcase.

"How long will you be gone?" I asked, knowing I wouldn't win this.

"I don't know, he didn't say. Maybe three months but could be longer."

Looks like I was going to be a single mom, after all. I just wouldn't have the financial burden on top of it. "What are you so upset about, anyway? I'm going to pay all the bills," he scoffed as he packed his last suitcase.

Holding my newborn, I watched as he drove away. I should've been relieved, but the message board that rejection threw in my face said, "REMINDER: You're not worth love, attention or time." My actions, or lack thereof, sent a message to Jerry that I would stay as long as he paid my way in life. Although I never made the conscious decision to stay for money, that was ultimately what I did. I didn't have to be loved or cared for, just bought.

When he threatened me, I stayed. When he flirted with women and didn't come home, I stayed. When he cursed at me, I stayed. When he drank himself into a rage and said things that broke me, I stayed! I sent a message that it was okay for him to do those things every time I chose to stay. I allowed him to treat me as worthless, and I tried harder to please him, hoping to be loved. I bowed to the lies of rejection every time the threats to throw me out came hurling my way.

I desired more than just the security of a roof over my head. I desired to be cherished. Money didn't bring happiness. It didn't make me feel loved or cherished, but it made me feel secure. I knew if I just kept my head down and my mouth shut, my son and I would not go without. I kept reasoning with myself, "Do what you have to do!"

The first year of my son's life was one of the hardest for me, but it also started to reshape my response to the abuse. Something about being a parent and not just looking out for my own well-being but the well-being of another helped me tap into a reserve of courage I didn't know I had. I wanted to be a better person and teach my son to be a good man. I was determined to be the best protector of this tiny human heart, as I could be. I spent that first year of motherhood contemplating how I should raise my child. I thought about what values I wanted to pass on and which ones I didn't.

Once the three months were up, Jerry announced we were moving to Wisconsin and we needed to be gone by the end of the week. There was no discussion, just orders for what I was going to do… or else! This time the "or else" was either I moved, or I would be left alone with no one to pay the bills. He also threatened to take our son away from me. I was young, naïve, scared and had no idea what my rights as a mother were. So, I started packing.

It didn't take long to see how he had been spending his time. He made a very close friend who liked to drink a lot. They would drink a pint of liquor while playing video games and grilling on the back porch of our apartment every night after work. He had already been a drinker, but it escalated into severe alcoholism. Without alcohol, he was easy to tick off. With alcohol, he was now a volcano erupting, with no warning. It was as if his meanness had been magnified. He frequently screamed obscenities and cursed at me. He got in my face and pushed me into walls without having the slightest idea why. He picked fights with me for fun! It was horrible, and then one day it became even more difficult than I could have imagined.

One evening, his friend came over for drinks. Our son, five months old at the time, was screaming and obviously having a rough teething day. I couldn't calm him down. He wasn't wet, he didn't need to eat, and he had taken a nap. I walked, rocked and tried to keep him quiet in the back bedroom, but nothing worked. I was in tears myself. After about an hour of this, Jerry came barreling into the room screaming, "Shut him up!" He then proceeded to get in our baby's face and scream, "SHUT UP!!"

I was mortified and my protect mode kicked in. I jumped up, while still holding our infant son in my arms, and pushed him out of the room. I had just crossed the threshold of holding back. He left while mumbling some crazy words as I slammed the door. Melting onto the floor in a puddle, I cuddled my baby close to my chest while soothing him as much as possible. I cried and vowed to him I would never let anyone hurt him... no matter what!

Staying out of Jerry's way worked for me most of the time, so that's what I did. Once a month, I made the journey to see my mother. By the time my son was born, she was no longer married to the verbally abusive Jim. Visiting was finally possible. I always wondered why I didn't just stay with her until I could figure something else out.

During my visits, I was given a schedule to call Jerry to be sure he woke up for work. He was always difficult to wake, and it often took calling for an hour before he answered. This was just another way to control me and the use of my time. The day before I was scheduled to leave to go back home, I called at the appointed time. However, this time there was no answer for over two hours. I started to worry and called his work. Maybe he had gotten up on his own and went ahead without my call?

Later that evening, I called his phone again with no answer. No one at work could get him to answer and they sent someone to our house to check on him. After calling him a few more times, I went to bed. I had a long trip the next day and needed rest. Enough was enough.

The next day, on our ten-hour journey home, I thought about what to do. I made up every possible scenario for what his excuse would be. The closer I got to home, the angrier I became. Only a few hours from arriving home, my phone rang. It was Jerry. He was acting strange and uncharacteristically nice. He asked how my trip was going and how the baby was doing, something he didn't normally care about. After short answers, I went straight to the source of my anger. "Where were you last night and why didn't you show up for your shift yesterday?"

He must've sensed my "I'm so done with you," tone. He meekly explained, "I went out drinking, drank too much, and passed out in the back of my friend's truck in the parking lot. He brought me home and got me on the couch and I guess I just slept through it. My boss was pretty upset with me, but Ben covered for me. It's no big deal. It's all good."

Really? It's all good? I don't think so. I had enough with the drinking and the irresponsible decisions he was making. I had enough with being his wake-up call, his booty call, and his punching bag! As he spoke, I made my decision. I was going home, packing all my things, and turning right back around. I wasn't raising my son with an abusive alcoholic. My reply was firm and short, "I'll come by the store when I get into town," and hung up.

When I arrived, Jerry was acting like a puppy who was in trouble for peeing on the floor. I couldn't figure out why, because I didn't think he cared. He was sweet to our son and offered to feed me. I remained cold to keep up my courage and rejected his offerings. I never told him I was leaving. I knew if I did, he would make sure I couldn't. But it was as if he already knew. We stayed only a few minutes and then headed to my house to pack.

I was home long enough to pack a couple of bags when the phone rang. I was in a hurry and sick to my stomach. I didn't want to have to do this! I had to remain angry though. It was the only way I would follow through. I answered the call, and it was him.

"What?!" I answered.

"Hey, I just wanted to tell you I'm sorry, and I am done with drinking. I won't do it anymore. I want you to pour out all the liquor in the house. I promise, I am done with it."

Okay, wait a minute. What was going on here? This was not the man I knew. The man I knew didn't apologize for anything and certainly didn't quit a bad habit on my behalf. His response made me soften my stance.

"How am I supposed to believe you? You aren't exactly honest with me," I questioned, "And I am not dumping your liquor. If you want to quit drinking, you're going to dump it yourself."

"I will," Jerry replied solemnly, "I will do it and in front of you! I just want to quit; I don't want to lose you Kathryn."

Once again, my mind was blown! He never spoke to me like that! Even though he guessed I was leaving, he didn't resort to his usual threats. I was so shocked; I thought I better give him a chance. After all, this behavior was what I had been waiting for.

He did what he said he'd do when he got home. No more alcohol. It wasn't long before we were packing to move back to Kentucky. He promised to find a job that would allow him to be home more. It appeared he was making a genuine effort.

For about a year, things were better for us. He had his moments, but much less often and severe. I could handle this. Our relationship seemed to grow into what I would consider real. It looked like a marriage, but without the wedding rings.

I've heard all good things must come to an end. The moment finally came when his old self resurfaced in full force. We were arguing about something, and he told me to shut up. When I said no, he started shoving me around the bathroom, into the door, and eventually into the bathtub where I almost fell onto our two-year-old.

Even though I was angry and felt small after all the pushing, I didn't even think about leaving this time. I just stayed out of his way and hoped it was a momentary relapse in behavior. Maybe it was my fault? I probably said something in a disrespectful tone. Yes, that's it. It was my fault, so I will just let it go. The next day came, and he acted as if nothing ever happened. He was back to his agreeable self. I guess we would just sweep that under the rug along with all the other junk we didn't want to look at.

I continued to reason with myself that things weren't that bad. If I played my cards right, he'd go back to treating me kindly or at least like a human being. He always gave me enough to think there was hope. Maybe he would be different this time? I walked around on eggshells, trying not to disturb the peace. Giving myself pep talks helped drowned out the hopelessness. *You can do this! You just need to keep trying, stick with it, try harder to please him and overlook it just one more time.*

The pain of the past still lingered, but he seemed normal in this moment. Ignoring all the pain, I stayed. I don't know where I got it from, but I have what I call "Hard Yes Syndrome." When I say yes, I commit fully to the yes. I said yes to this relationship so many times. I was determined to make it work. I had this tenacious, sheer fire determination to stick with it, even if it made me miserable. If I am honest, that stick-to-it mentality wasn't a commendable attribute in this situation. This mentality kept me trapped for far too long. I made fear-based choices and accepted lies I believed were truth.

You are not enough, will never be enough, and you are nothing without him.

Fear said, "You can't do this without him," and reminded me that I had no way out. I had agreed with fear so much that there never seemed to be an option to step out into freedom.

I was terrified of change and the unknown. I might fail if I were brave enough to leave. By moving out, I would have to give up all the comforts I'd gotten used to. I was terrified of being stranded with no one to help me. More importantly, I was afraid that no one would ever want me and I would be alone. When I looked in the mirror, I saw someone no one would ever consider loving. I felt used up and unworthy.

7

STICKS AND STONES MAY BREAK MY BONES

Someone once told me that doing the same thing repeatedly while expecting different results is the definition of insanity. I felt like the poster child because I just kept allowing the same old thing to happen and hoping for a different outcome! I was not yet at a place where the pain of change was greater than the pain of staying the same.

Four years later, I was pregnant again, this time with a beautiful baby girl. I was growing from a teen to a woman and I began seeing things differently. As time went on, I became more opinionated and less afraid. It was time to think about being a better example for my children. I thought it wasn't right for me to stay in this relationship and not be married. I wanted my children to have parents who were married. I also began to feel a tug in my heart toward God. I yearned for something better and hoped God would be the answer.

I gathered enough courage to talk to Jerry about my thoughts. Until then, we hadn't discussed God, other than whether we believed in Him. To my surprise, he agreed to try attending church. I noticed how he watched other men there and for the first time, I realized that I wasn't the only one who didn't have the best examples growing up. No wonder it was so difficult!

We learned how God expected us to live and how he wanted us to treat one another. It embarrassed me that we were living together, unmarried, while I was pregnant. I was even more ashamed when I went to church. One day, we stopped by to meet the pastor after the service. Jerry introduced me to him as "his wife, Kathryn," to which I immediately replied without thinking, "Well, we're not married. I'm his girlfriend."

I was six months pregnant. I expected to be ushered to the door and asked to never to come back. To my surprise, no guards showed up to drag us to the exit. Instead, we were showered with love and acceptance. Pastor Ben even invited us to meet him later that afternoon to get to know us better.

During our meeting, he asked us to share our story with him. That was difficult. No one had ever asked us that before. Our story wasn't one of boy meets girl, they fall in love and live happily ever after. No part of our journey was picture perfect or romantic. I shared the superficial details about how it had not always been easy.

We had a son and another baby on the way that we wanted to be a good example for. Pastor Ben explained how God saw marriage, why it was important, and that we should consider getting married as soon as possible or separate.

I wanted to please God, and I didn't want to have another baby out of wedlock. I hadn't realized the importance of marriage until that day, and I was ready to do whatever it took to get it right. We both were. This was a quick decision that we felt certain was the right thing to do. A few short weeks later, I waddled down the aisle toward Jerry. I hoped taking this step would fix everything.

After we brought our daughter home, things were wonderful. We all settled into our new routines, and Jerry was more involved in the parenting process. It wasn't perfect, but noticeably better. Going to church regularly was helping. He was softening and becoming more peaceful and less angry, but I could never tell if this was the time those changes would stick. I hoped for the best. For a while, things changed. That was the longest stretch of calm I can remember. Unfortunately, it didn't last.

When everything was good, it was like a once in a lifetime vacation. When you are there, everything else melts away. All responsibilities and routines are gone. Reality becomes a distant memory as you feel the joy of being in a place you've always dreamed of relaxing in. You soak up the sun and take in the views.

While you're there, you even talk about moving someday. "If I lived here, noting else would matter. I could be this happy for the rest of my life."

Then comes the moment when you have to leave your dream destination. It's time to go back to the reality of life. Once you return, you find everything the way you left it, except maybe a little dustier. It's back to the grind and the same old, same old. Things don't look as colorful as they did before. The first week back is full of busyness as you try to get things in order: laundry done, groceries restocked (since you left your chef in paradise), the house dusted and bills back on track. It's a little sad, right?

Our highs were like this. They were temporary and left me wishing I could live in that moment forever. The lows of being back in reality were like wandering in a dark valley, wondering where the sun went and if there was a way out of it.

One of the hardest things I have ever done in my life is to have one foot in the door of our relationship and one foot out. It feels like being torn in two. I wanted to be all in, but it was difficult. My heart wanted it to work, but my head kept screaming, "Get OUT!" I was in too far now to turn back. I had made the choice to marry him, and we had children. I had to stay now, right?

I continued trudging ahead, hoping, waiting and wishing for change. Abuse is a very tricky thing. There is a cycle that occurs, one

I was not even aware of at the moment. It feels like being stuck in a hamster wheel. I was running in a circle but never seemed to get anywhere.

In 1979, Dr. Lenore Walker called this the "Cycle of Violence." I am going to use the term abuse vs violence because violence can lead someone to only focus on the physical side of abuse. Walker looked at the repetitive nature of the perpetrator's actions and how it hinders a victim's ability to leave an abusive relationship. Her theory shows how the behavior of a perpetrator can change from one end of the spectrum to another. This behavior makes it difficult for a woman to leave. I wish I would have seen this information a lot sooner.[1]

Dr. Walker explains the cycle in four phases. I used my own situation to fill in this flow chart while keeping the original name of each phase the same.

Phase 1: Tension-building

- This is the uncertain phase where I hoped things would remain calm. I was always afraid of what would happen if they didn't. I tiptoed around as quietly as possible to keep from disrupting the peace.

- Tension builds, and eventually I'd say or do something wrong. The end result looked like what happens when the reactor button gets pushed on a time bomb.

Phase 2: Acute Explosion

- This is usually when the worst would happen. Jerry would rage, yell, call me names, and remind me of my helplessness when we first met and how much I needed him. He would sometimes take my cell phone, keys, and wallet. He used mind games, fear, and taking things from me to control and maintain power. While in defeat mode, I shut down completely. I could not rationalize or reason with him. My only choice was to get quiet and hope it would be over soon.

Phase 3: The Honeymoon

- Then came the pursuit. My complete silence wasn't a tactic to make him pay, but one to protect myself. Jerry saw it as a sign of punishment. He'd slink around like a puppy who'd been scolded for pulling out the trash in the kitchen. He wouldn't apologize but I could tell he felt bad. Instead of acknowledging his wrong actions, he helped me around the house while making random comments. He would say things like "sure is a nice day today" or "I was thinking about planting some bushes this morning". Flowers would show up that were meant to make all the pain go away. I saw them as a "let's call this good" gesture.

Eventually, I would bring up the last attack and make sure he knew flowers would not cut it. I didn't like being treated that way. There was still no apology, but at least he promised he'd never do it again.

He wouldn't take responsibility for his actions. Instead, he would blame them on lack of sleep, his boss, or sometimes even me.

There would be a complete personality change. For the next week or so, he would be kinder and more attentive to me. I was relieved that he was acting better, yet I was still hurt by the lack of closure. Okay, let's try again.

As I got older, courage rose within me. I was changing. I cared about myself more and less about his opinion or his reactions. I had children to consider in all of this. What kind of example was I showing them? Didn't I want them to value and respect me? Then I certainly should expect the same from their father. I didn't always get it, but at least I stood up for myself more. I became more verbal, pointing out the things I could no longer keep silent about.

The times when things were better gave me enough hope to keep going when they weren't. When I refer to bad times, I don't mean not agreeing and having silly arguments. No, I mean the times when Jerry would push me, curse at me and call me horrible names. The times when I found explicit texts and emails he sent to other women. Sometimes he'd get drunk and watch pornography in the middle of the afternoon on our television just to remind me whose house this was. Those were the bad times.

When bad things happened at the age of seventeen, I quietly tried to ignore them. However, the longer I lived this way, the harder it was to keep quiet. Eventually, the things I experienced and the way I was treated didn't seem as scary. Now, they just became annoying, and I was getting fed up with the same old cycle. I considered the idea that maybe he wouldn't change after all, that this was just how it was going to be. I stopped crying about things, telling myself to either do something about it or shut up. Gradually, I developed thick skin. Things still hurt, but I hid them, even from myself. I bitterly ignored the pain, shoving it to the deepest parts of my sad and angry heart.

Sticks and stones may break my bones, but words will never hurt me... right? Well, whoever said that was incredibly misinformed! Words hurt! I can't count the number of times I wished he would just break a bone, leave my heart out of it, and stop playing with my mind.

8

IT STARTED AT THE EVENT

"Stay alert! Watch out for your great enemy, the devil.
He prowls around like a roaring lion, looking for
someone to devour." (1 Peter 5:8 NLT)

Our enemy desires to cause real and lasting harm. Peter warns us of this! Satan seeks to leave us as weak and ineffective as possible to keep us from walking in the goodness and promises of God. He uses situations and circumstances to shake our faith, making way for fear to rule our lives. Satan knows the place with our Father is secured through Christ Jesus (Ephesians 1:13-14). The enemy just doesn't want us to know it! He feeds us lies to try to convince us that God is not good, that we are not His, loved and bought with a great price. If the enemy can get us to believe we aren't valuable, then we won't believe we're cared for by the one who created us.

This was part of my problem. A big part actually. Even though I had accepted Jesus Christ as my savior at a young age, I never fully understood what that meant. Satan seized every opportunity to interject lies, causing doubt about who I really was. He patiently observed how I responded to situations, listened to what I said about myself, and watched how I allowed others to treat me. Like a lion, Satan stalks his prey and attacks us in a very strategic manner.

Usually, herd animals will keep their young or wounded in the center of the group for protection from predators. If one wanders outside of the herd, they are now an open target. The predator watches and waits, hidden in the shadows until he sees his opportunity. Then he goes in for the kill! Likewise, the enemy of our soul watches and waits for the very moment when we decide to leave the safety of our covering. He strikes when we are alone, vulnerable, weak, and wounded.

I didn't have a herd in my life to protect me while I was young in the Lord. I was an open target. I couldn't walk in the fullness of God's promises because I didn't even know what they were. As I became an adult, I still didn't have a herd. I was a loner. If someone tried to get close, I shut it down.

I was now wounded and limping along, but still felt I needed to go at it alone. I saw no value in community with others. "Who needs friends?" I told myself, "Not me." Little did I realize the importance of having someone to lift me up and speak truth to me. Wandering around alone in life without a powerful community around me was the very weapon Satan used for so long to keep me in my prison cell. I was exactly where he wanted me to be: isolated, wounded and unaware.

Our family didn't stay somewhere long enough to build community, make friends, and grow roots. This was fine with me since I wasn't interested in inviting anyone into the reality and embarrassment of my life. That was all about to change.

I'd dreamed of living in California since I was a little girl. I wanted to move to Los Angeles and open a coffee shop, then start a chain of coffee shops and live out the rest of my days as a millionaire. I even drew up my own plans for the mansion I was going to build. Funny how life ended up and how impossible those dreams now seemed. I did eventually make it to California, but for other reasons. Even though I had abandoned my coffee shop dream, I was still elated to be there.

I enjoyed being a stay-at-home mom, but I knew I had to find a job. It was time to take a stand and create some sort of independence for myself. I was frustrated with my life and tired of fighting for change. I wanted to quit, but I had no money, no car, no job... nothing. Loneliness was consuming me. I couldn't keep listening to myself anymore. I needed an outside perspective. I needed a friend.

So I called my grandma.

My grandma was the only person I can remember who took an interest in me when I was growing up. She wrote me letters all throughout my childhood even though she lived far away. Her visits were my happiest memories. Grandma liked to hug and play with my hair. She liked it when I sat with her and talked. When she was around, I felt seen and safe because I knew the man I called dad wouldn't bother me while she was there.

When I decided to leave my mother's house at fifteen, communication with my grandma stopped for a long time. We didn't talk anymore. It wasn't her fault; it was mine. I thought she would be mad at me. She always told me to be a good girl and help my mom. I didn't want to be honest and tell her why I had left my mom and siblings. I didn't want to tell her how things were at home. After I left, I assumed she saw me as a bad girl who didn't help her mom like she was supposed to. I felt I had let her down and so I hid for years.

After being alone in California for over a year, I picked up the phone and hoped she would talk to me. I shouldn't have been surprised, but I was. On the other end of the phone was a voice filled with love. She was very glad to hear from me.

We had a lot of catching up to do! She asked me question after question, and I answered them honestly. It was tough, but I felt compelled to share with her what happened and why. I told her about my situation with Jerry and everything else that had happened. Relief swept over me as we chatted that day.

Before we hung up the phone, she gave me a piece of advice I will never forget. She said, "Honey, listen. You need to be smart. No young lady should ever be without a little nest egg of her own. You need to be putting money back that he isn't aware of in case of emergencies. Don't ever be in a place of complete dependence on him or you will be stuck forever. Get a job and start putting money aside now, just in case. I am not saying you will need it, but always have a backup plan Katyroo. Okay?"

Why hadn't I thought of that?! She shared how she had done that very thing as a young woman. If it was good enough for her, it was good enough for me. I will always be glad I picked up the phone that day because it set in motion a call to action in my life. Those next few months, we called each other and talked often. I didn't know it then, but if I had remained ashamed to call, I would have missed my chance altogether. It wasn't long after we reconnected she went to be with Jesus.

After my grandmother passed, I realized the importance of relationships like never before. I missed our talks and started to look for a friend.

One of the driving factors of our move was a multi-level

marketing business Jerry believed would be his ticket to millionaire status. I had no actual part in the business, but I was expected to attend events with him. My role was to sit still and look pretty. I went to home meetings and leadership training seminars with him. Little did I know how much my life would be changed through attending the meetings, listening to the trainings on tape, and reading the books we were given every month. I was like a dry sponge soaking up water. I needed this lifeline more than I ever realized to teach me life principles and help me shed a few of my old, negative thought patterns and beliefs.

After years of being filled with leadership development and training, I believed some of the empowering thoughts that were taught. Although I knew I could never flourish under Jerry's thumb, I gained the confidence I needed to step out of my shell and fulfill my desire to lead, love and be in community with others.

God used this season of my life to set up a series of what I call checkpoint people who would each lead me to learn a distinct part of His character. One such checkpoint person was Ruby. We met in a lobby of a leadership seminar. She looked bored, and I had been practicing my newfound people skills, so I sparked up a conversation. This was a big deal for a quiet, "don't speak unless spoken to" girl from Kentucky. With all the confidence I could muster, I made eye contact, smiled, and began a casual conversation.

I practiced asking a question with a question and then our casual talks soon formed a friendship.

She invited me to come to church with her family. Since moving, we hadn't connected to a church yet, so I was glad to go. Naturally, Ruby assumed I was on the same level as she was since I carried the Christian title, but unfortunately this wasn't the case. I did the church thing and checked it off for the week, but somehow I never learned I could have a relationship with God; talk with him, walk with him and know him intimately.

Growing up, one of the many things my mother was good at was getting us to church camps. She tried to make sure we were exposed to God. I'll always be thankful she sent me when she could. Not only did it give me a week away from abuse, but I got to experience what childhood was supposed to be like during those weeks. After a full day of swimming, hiking, and games, all the kids would come together for chapel before our nightly camp fire. Typically, I zoned out, staring at the back of the boy's head in front of me that I had a crush on. At the end of the very last church camp I was to attend as a child, something life changing happened.

During chapel, there was a story woven together in such a fascinating way that I hung on every word. This loving God who wanted me so much that He would send His only son to Earth to live a perfect life and die as a perfect sacrifice for my sin intrigued me. I felt dirty because of what was happening to me. But this preacher said I could be made clean if I believed Jesus was my savior and trusted He could wash all my uncleanliness away. At the end of the story, the preacher gave an altar call that went something like this: "If you want to know the love of Jesus and feel love like you have never felt before, raise your hand and pray this prayer after me." My hand shot up before my mind could respond! As the pastor prayed, I felt what I can only describe as a hug in my heart. At that moment, I felt love like never before.

Even though I felt that love once, I thought it was contingent on my behavior and performance. I viewed my relationship with God the same way I did with my grandmother. I was convinced He must be disappointed in me so I chose to stay away.

I was afraid of being wrong about His unfailing love and doubted that God cared more about who I was than what I had done. I doubted His goodness and mercy. I doubted he wanted me around since I had doubted Him. That's a lot of doubt!

The truth was, He was always wooing me to Himself. He kept me under His wing of protection while I was making unwise choices. While I was running the other way, He was right there waiting for me to turn around and see Him with arms wide open, ready to receive His daughter. No strings attached, no hoops to jump through, no other reason than just because I was His. Back then, I wasn't aware He was always with me, knew me intimately, and cared about what I cared about. I didn't realize that He wept when I wept and caught every tear. That He laughed when I laughed and wanted me to be filled with joy unimaginable. He wanted me to be free from the bondage of my bad choices and wrong mindsets. I was unaware that God could heal my heart and that He even wanted to.

This is why isolation is so dangerous. We need to be connected to others who will speak truth and life to us. We need others to help us see our blind spots and encourage us to grow. If we are alone and without fellowship with other believers, we are available prey for the devil. As I stated earlier, he seeks whom he may devour. Satan did all he could to keep me from others who could help me out of the mud pit and point me safely through the minefield.

I was starving spiritually. Instead of feeding myself from the Word, I needed others to spoon feed me the truth. This was primarily because I didn't understand it. God knew I would not do it on my own, so he sent a friend who would point me to Him.

The first time I went to church with Ruby was a new experience for me. There was a full band on stage and people were raising their hands while they sang, dancing and shouting Hallelujah. I didn't know how to feel about the freedom of expression I witnessed that day. I debated going back, but I was curious to find out what they seemed to have that I clearly did not.

There was something drawing me. I wanted my kids to experience God, and I didn't know enough to lead them to Him myself. I wanted Jerry to go with us, but he refused, so we went without him. Even though I fought the urge to stay home every Sunday for six months, I kept going. But no matter how long I attended, I couldn't shake the uncomfortable feeling that wrenched in my stomach every time I walked in the door.

I was angry my life didn't look like everyone else's, or at least how I perceived their lives to look. I felt rejected and judged, although no one made me feel this way. I realize now that it was my own issues, and the condemner of my soul was trying to get me to stay away. I wouldn't connect with anyone. People tried to reach out to me, but I refused to let them in. My routine was to make my escape as soon as the altar call began. I was the first to the nursery to grab my kids and run out the door before anyone could stop me to ask how I was. I was so embarrassed about my life and the anger raging within me.

Change leads to change, which at times is uncomfortable, and this was exactly what I was experiencing. There was a change happening, but it was so subtle I didn't recognize it as that. I kept moving through the discomfort and God worked within me, leading me out of my self-developed defense mechanisms. He was setting me up to decide if I wanted to leave the emotional isolation behind that I used to protect myself for so long. He wanted to heal my brokenness and become my defender, but it was up to me to choose.

One afternoon, in the middle of a routine day caring for my two small children, my phone rang. Juggling my daughter on one hip and lunch for my son I was less than thrilled that my phone was ringing. Even so, I answered. On the other end of the phone was the sweet voice of my friend Ruby. I could feel my spirit lift. I was so glad I took the time to pick up the call. The conversation started with normal small talk but quickly changed course. This was part of that "change that creates change" thing. It was unexpected and completely took me by surprise.

I could tell she was nervous when she began speaking. Her first syllable drawn out, "Sooooo, I know this is going to sound crazy and if you don't want to, it's ok, but I really feel like God is asking me to disciple you. Would you be okay with that?" I didn't even understand what discipleship was. After she explained, I knew immediately that I needed it.

This one act of obedience by my sweet friend was a game changer in my life. Hindsight really is 20/20. As I look back, this was the beginning of my journey to healing and wholeness. Even though there were still more years of pain, sadness, anger and abuse, there was hope and a reshaping taking place in the very depths of my soul. Ruby had two small children at home like I did, and yet, she made it work. She did what she felt like the Lord had asked her to do and it forever left a footprint in my life that has rippled beyond what I could ever imagine.

Over the next twelve weeks, Ruby and I went through a discipleship curriculum together remotely. She and I read the lesson on our own during the week. I did the homework and wrote down anything I didn't understand. Every Friday afternoon during nap time, we called each other to go through that week's lesson. She graciously gave me as much time as I needed to ask questions, and boy did I have questions. She helped me understand who Jesus really was when He walked the Earth, what He did for me on the cross and who He is in my life daily. She patiently explained things I felt like I should have already known.

In the past, when I attempted to read the Bible, it was hard for me to understand. I got frustrated and put it down often. I didn't see how relevant it was to me. These were just a bunch of stories of dead people anyway, right? What does any of this have to do with me? I didn't get it because I was looking at it all wrong. I had never been told the Word was alive and relevant today. If something is alive, it's breathing, right? I hadn't seen it that way, so I wasn't allowing the Word to breathe on me. Ruby helped me understand this. I bought a Bible that I could understand and studied it with her help.

During this time of discipleship, I spent a lot of time outdoors on the phone. My neighbor, Joyce, usually sat outside on her patio during the same times I chatted with Ruby about Jesus. One afternoon, after hanging up from my weekly conversation, Joyce came over to invite me to join a mom's group at a local church. It was only ten minutes from my apartment, and she offered to drive. Sure, what could it hurt? I was bored on Tuesdays, anyway. I didn't know Joyce well, but her invitation was a God set up that I wouldn't recognize until later.

Joyce didn't attend this church, or any other. She was like me; a mom who needed to get out of the house occasionally, so she joined. After going for a season, I realized I felt comfortable in the building and had made some connections with other ladies. It was closer to home than the church I went to with Ruby, so I attended a Saturday evening service. If I didn't like it, I could still go to my church on Sunday morning. It was an enormous church compared to the smaller one I usually attended. I felt as though I could get lost in the crowd. I could slip in and out unnoticed.

I started attending Faith Fellowship in the hopes that not knowing anyone would be an incentive for Jerry to come with me. After we were married, we quit going to church together. Once we moved to California, we planned to get back into the routine together, however it didn't happen that way. This was okay with me at first, but it became increasingly hard to battle feeling alone. It often distracted me noticing the couples all over the room during each service. I started longing for what others seemed to have and wished my husband would go to church with me.

Satan used this open door to attack me. He whispered lies to keep me from continuing to go to church. "Don't you want to stop feeling so uncomfortable? You don't belong here. Just stay home, it's easier. Why are you doing this to yourself?" Even though I heard the thoughts beckoning surrender, I kept going. I sulked many times while I was there and thought of possible excuses for why I should get up and leave, but something always kept me right in my seat.

9

WHATEVER MEANS NECESSARY

Building a deep relationship with anyone takes time. The same is true of our relationship with God. I am still getting to know Him. He is always inviting me to come closer. He actively pursues me. His love for me never gives up or grows weary of my running. God never got fed up and washed His hands of me because of my poor choices. He loved me so much that He was willing to extend infinite patience while I slowly learned to trust Him.

In order to learn who I am, I had to first learn who He is, all three parts! God the Father, God the Son and God the Holy Spirit. Ruby was the first checkpoint on my journey, teaching me more about Jesus. God is so faithful to set up divine appointments! The next appointment would lead me to a new level of healing in my heart and greater intimacy with God.

I continued going to Faith Fellowship. It didn't take long to fall in love with the church. People were welcoming, and no one seemed to mind that I was always alone. I realized people were a lot less interested in why than I imagined, and no one was judging me but me!

I soaked up every moment as I discovered new things about God's promises. Pastors shared about topics I'd never heard before. I watched in amazement as pastors gave prophetic words of healing, and painted the most vivid pictures of the stories in God's Word. This church became my happy place. I felt like I was a part of something bigger than me for the first time in my life.

I volunteered to serve at the annual summer Vacation Bible School. I discovered I really enjoyed organizing events with a team. I had never been a part of anything like this and I was so excited to experience this with my kids! During VBS, my son, David, kept telling me about his new friend, Trey. All week he kept asking if we could arrange a play date to which my reply was always, "Sure honey, but I don't know his mommy and I would need to meet her first."

During parent pickup on the very last day, he and his new friend came running in from outside, sweaty and out of breath, to catch me before I left. "Mom! Trey's mom is outside to meet you. She said we could have a play date!"

Trey ushered me over to his mother, Michelle, and introduced me. I instantly liked her. She was radiant and peaceful. Her smile said, "You're important!" and her eyes were so loving and genuine. We didn't talk long, but long enough to exchange numbers with the promise to set up that play date!

Our first play date would be that very next week. Michelle seemed to care so genuinely about me from the very first conversation. There was a noticeable difference in this woman, and that intrigued me. She wanted to know my story and was the best listener. I answered most of her questions with the shiniest answers I could conjure up. However, Michelle was great at asking deeper, more detailed questions that left me no room to gloss over anything. I wanted to hide the truth and pretend to be normal. And then came the dreaded questions about my marriage. It was always hard to talk about this subject.

Michelle seemed as if she had hearts popping up around her and maybe even bluebirds singing in the distance as she anticipated my response. This was going to be difficult because Jerry and I had no Cinderella love story.

It was awkward for me to answer these questions. I didn't have that swooning love in my heart she was hoping to hear. "How long have you been married?" she asked.

Slowly I answered, "Well, only two years. We were living unmarried for seven years." Insert awkward silence.

How did you meet?" She responded with excited anticipation in her voice for the story of great romance to unravel in front of her.

My stomach ached. "I was homeless and seventeen, so he let me move in with him. Oh, did I mention he was my boss?" Clearly this wasn't going the way she hoped. She asked me a bit about my homeless story and after answering as briefly as I could, we continued talking.

"Well, what do you all do for fun?" she asked. But I wish she hadn't.

"My husband plays video games and works a lot. I take care of the kids and enjoy doing that. We don't really get out together to do things."

That last question hurt my heart to answer more than I care to admit. I dreamed of having what other couples did. Intentional time together. Time devoted to conversation and fun. Instead, I was the maid, nanny and an object to be called upon when he had a need. He pulled me out of his back pocket when he wanted to show me off, but otherwise invisible. We didn't date before marriage. I never set a standard for that type of thing. So, it was no different after we were married.

Marriage wasn't my favorite topic, so I just brushed it off. My brief answers gave away my eagerness to change the subject. She was gracious in moving the conversation along to something else. I didn't want to let her in all the way, but just enough. She made me feel so loved the entire time I was with her. It was as if we weren't complete strangers just hanging out because our kids wanted to play together. I left that day feeling valued. This was the only time I spent with her before the worst came.

I was married to someone who had an addictive personality. Whatever he did, he was immersed in it. One of his many addictions was video games. It was not just a hobby for him, but every free moment they consumed him. He got very little sleep during his work week because he stayed up to play until the early morning hours.

He always had to "just finish this one last campaign." The games he chose were violent first-person shooter style. He enjoyed playing them online so he could completely disappear from reality. I would have to leave the house or stay outside on the days he was off work. I didn't want the children in his way or they would get screamed at for standing in front of the game he loved so much.

We only had one TV in our small apartment. At night, I would put the children to bed and lay in my bedroom listening to him yell curse words and other obscenities to his teammates. When I could take it no more, I'd ask him to keep it down but to no avail. Most of the time, I think it made him get even louder.

This was especially hard for me one night as I woke up multiple times from his shouting. After laying in the bed frustrated at 2am, I decided I had enough. Getting out of bed, breathing deeply as I walked down the stairs, I gathered up my courage and sat next to him on the couch. As always, he acted as if I wasn't even in the room. After a few minutes went by, with my heart beating out of my chest, I asked when he would come to bed. His response was much like the ones I had heard in the past. "When I feel like it, Kathryn."

Anger raged in me, but I felt helpless to change anything at the moment, until I had the idea to turn off the video game. Bravely, I stepped up to the video game console and pushed the off button. I had never done anything like this before, although I had dreamed about it.

The next thing I knew, a controller was flying across the room at me. I was able to dodge it and ran back to the couch, thinking, *what did I just do?* He was yelling at me, so to calm him, I reached out and put my hand on his shoulder. When I did, he turned and lunged at me, knocking me onto my back. With his knees on my shoulders and his body on my chest, he gripped my throat with one hand and began choking me.

Terrified and struggling to breathe, I couldn't even fight. I lay stunned, pinned to the couch, and a sickening thought crossed my mind. He was going to kill me. As my face felt like it was swelling and the pressure in my ears felt like a balloon about to explode, he released me. My throat was on fire as I gasped for air.

I lay still for a long time, feeling shocked, helpless, and small. I could not respond. I didn't know how to react or what to do. I only remember thinking I had to keep quiet so I wouldn't wake the children. I couldn't bear the thought of them seeing or hearing what happened. After he got off my chest, he went straight outside to smoke without another word.

After a few minutes, he stormed back inside. By this time, I had made my way up to a seated position. Still trying to catch my breath, he yelled, "Look what you made me do Kathryn, you're so stupid."

As he rummaged through my purse looking for my phone and wallet, he continued about how I would not put him in jail like his ex-girlfriend. Until that moment, I didn't think to call the police. I couldn't think clearly about anything. After getting what he wanted, he stormed back to the living room, turned his Xbox on, picked up his headset and began apologizing to the strangers he played online with explaining, "I had to take care of something."

Just as fast as it happened, it was over.

Defeated, I got up and mindlessly wandered to the back porch to sit in the dark and try to process what just happened. I felt something sweep over me that differed completely from the angry undercurrent

I lived with. This was a tsunami of sorrow and hopelessness I never saw coming.

When I was a child, the enemy tried taking me out as an infant with a diagnosis of failure to thrive and pneumonia. At three months old, the doctor's report read, "Stopped breathing all together. Intubated at 11:06am." As a child, the enemy tried to convince me to succumb to the hopelessness of life and kill myself. Now he was using my husband to choke out my very breath in an attempt to keep me from ever finding out what I was called to do. He would not stop until he silenced my life and my purpose.

The next day was a very dark day. I slept little and when I woke up, the bathroom mirror revealed an ugly reminder of the events of that early morning. I had his entire handprint around my neck and bruises on my arms. All I could do was cry as I examined my body.

Exhausted and numb, I robotically took care of my little one's needs. I felt like a zombie, walking, but dead. I sat outside on my patio wondering what to do most of the morning. I wanted to ignore it and pretend it didn't happen, but I couldn't. I didn't want to talk to anyone, yet I knew I needed to. Who should I call? What could I do?

Relying on family was not in the cards, so I reached out to my new friend Michelle. She seemed wise and maybe she'd have some encouragement for me to keep holding on. The conversation was as awkward as you might imagine. I began with, "I know you don't really know me, but I have to talk to someone. I need to just get this out."

I shared how I hadn't been honest about my marriage and there was great abuse as I shared about the events of the early morning. After praying with me, she told me about a local, domestic violence outreach where I could seek help.

After hanging up the phone with her, I reached out to this place that dealt with battered women and children. Nervously, I asked if I could talk to someone and get help with what just happened to me. They asked me to come in right away. In my mind, I was going to get counseling to help me deal with the immense sadness I was feeling. I didn't know they could see me right away; I was relieved they could get me in so quickly. Thankfully, Jerry left my phone and wallet on the kitchen counter before he left that day.

Upon arriving at this center, I was ushered into a room to talk with a counselor. She struck up some small talk about my kids to make me comfortable. It wasn't long before she noticed the marks on my neck that I'd tried covering with makeup that morning. She asked me about them and without warning; I broke down and sobbed right there in front of a complete stranger. I explained the events of the night before and asked for help to get over my sadness about it.

After a few minutes, a female police officer entered the room. *What was she doing here?* Regret and fear gripped me. I remember saying over and over, "I didn't come here for this. I only wanted to talk. I don't want him to go to jail, he is going to be so mad." The officer explained that this was not okay and I would be safe from now on if I wanted to be. She explained how the children and I could be in a safe place, away from the home, while they arrested him. Uncertainty and fear were at the forefront of my mind, but there was a certain relief I felt knowing I could be free… no wait, I AM free. This was over… but now what?

I spent the next few days adjusting to the peace and quiet in the house. I tried to keep moving on as though nothing was different. I knew I needed to figure out how to pay the bills, but I couldn't seem to think straight about anything. Panic would sweep over me in waves without warning.

Day three of my newfound freedom did not differ from day one and two. As I mindlessly went on with household chores, putting one foot in front of the other while reminding myself to just breathe, I carried a load of newly folded laundry upstairs. Thoughts of anger and fear flooded my mind as I remembered the event of a few evenings ago. Right before I reached the top, I heard God say, "Forgive Him."

I halted my assent and frustratingly replied, "WHAT! You want me to forgive him?"

This was the first time I knew I heard from God. Now, I am sure He spoke to me before, but I wasn't really listening. And even if I thought it might have been God, I usually dismissed it as my own thoughts. This time, however, I knew without a doubt it was the Lord speaking. I wouldn't have told myself to forgive him. I wanted to be free of him! My understanding of forgiveness was that if I forgave, I was asking for punishment and pain. How could God ask me to forgive this man who had hurt me so much?

Had I listened further in that moment, He probably would have revealed more to me. Instead, I stomped up the rest of the stairs, fell on my bedroom floor and sobbed, wondering why I had been told to forgive him. Anger raged in my heart as I tried to understand. I couldn't imagine how I would do something like this or why I should. All I knew was God said it.

What I didn't realize was that forgiving someone is an act of surrender to the true Judge and King of the Universe. Forgiveness is more for me than it is for the other person. I thought forgiveness meant saying that it was ok to allow the offender back into my life. Had I listened longer that day and talked to God further, I would have known God didn't say let him back in. He only said, "FORGIVE HIM."

Shortly after being bailed out of jail, Jerry reached out to me several times, begging to come home and work it out. These pleas were followed by grand promises that things would be different this time. After hearing I should forgive him, I agreed to meet to discuss things. There were big promises to never again play the video game he blamed for his rage. He even broke it into pieces in front of me. He promised to be better, to be faithful, to treat me kind, to pay attention to his family. So, I agreed to try again.

I hoped this would be the change I had waited so long to see. I couldn't help but wonder, what if this was the time when he meant it and I refused to allow him to show me he was different? Things were better, but not for long. He hadn't experienced true transformation. He did the right things long enough to get me back into a place of dependency on him. Then he would get comfortable and fall back into the same old routines. I hadn't yet learned that behavior modification is not heart transformation.

Soon after moving back in and getting the charges dropped, Jerry bought the same game he vowed to never play again, and we were in the same place we were before. Except he was careful not to be physically violent with me. Sometimes, I almost wished he would hit me and get it over with rather than continue the verbal abuse.

Abuse cuts deep into a person's core and causes lasting damage that is hard to clean up. The verbal and emotional abuse caused me to feel as though I had been in a boxing ring for hours with the toughest boxer you can imagine. I felt like this boxer was just punching me until I couldn't see or think straight. It left me exhausted and unable to fight. The emotional and verbal abuse clouded my thinking and made me bitter and angry. I was angry at myself for choosing this again and bitter at him for being so mean and dishonest. Again!

On top of the verbal beatings from him, I beat myself up 24/7. This was my fault! I blamed myself for being a coward. I didn't know how to live on the other side of fear; free and believing God was my true provision. I didn't trust God because I didn't know His character... yet. Instead, I went back into my cell and waited with the door wide open.

10

DON'T YOU KNOW WHO I AM?

Thankfully, Michelle continued to reach out to me and I started spending a lot of time with her. I'd drive the 30 minutes to her house and spend the afternoon with her anytime she offered. Being with her made me feel calm and cared for. She carried peace I didn't know. I wanted to be near her, just to feel that peace for even a moment.

I spent afternoons on her couch pouring my heart out. She was a safe place to finally release what I had held in for so long. She quietly listened with love in her eyes while I complained about my decisions. There was never a time when I felt as though I was too much for her or that she didn't care.

I wanted what she had. Not her nice house, her income, her beautiful patio furniture or her life... only the peace she carried.

Even though chaos was all around me, time stood still and my worries seemed small when I was with her.

After a couple of visits, she asked some questions that made me uncomfortable in a new way. "What's your prayer life look like right now? Do you pray in the Spirit? Do you know who the Holy Spirit is?" the answers to those questions were embarrassing and frustrating at the same time.

Until this point in my life, I spent little time in prayer. What time I spent praying consisted of complaints. There were no two-way conversations happening where I truly listened to what God wanted to say. I spent years of my life in a church building, yet didn't realize the importance of prayer or even how to pray.

I had only just learned who Jesus really was. I had faith that He died for my sins and was the sacrifice for all of mankind. Because of God the Son, I believed I had eternal life with God the Father in Heaven. It was not a problem to believe that God created the world in six days and all of humanity was His idea. However, I didn't have faith to believe that I could be filled with God, the Holy Spirit. After all, why would He want to live in me?

I believed nothing about me was worthy of His presence, and certainly not His power (Acts 1:8, Ephesians 3:16, Romans 6:10-11, Matthew 10:6, Mark 16:15, Luke 9:1).

I hadn't learned much about the Holy Spirit yet. Just a month before meeting with Michelle, my pastor taught a series on The Holy Spirit. I listened with great interest as he explained that He is our guide, our inner voice, our friend, and comforter. He speaks to us and helps us navigate through this life. Pastor Kirk explained that when we are filled with the Holy Spirit, we receive the fruit of the Spirit; love, joy, peace, patience, kindness, goodness, faithfulness, gentleness, and self-control. I wanted all of that, but especially joy.

He explained how being filled with the Holy Spirit meant I would be filled with His power and God would dwell within me. At the end of the service, there was a call to action for anyone who wanted to be filled with The Holy Spirit. My hand darted up... me... oh, oh, pick me! We were asked to stand as a sign that we wanted to receive this filling of the Spirit of God. I stood along with many others, and I received the baptism of the Holy Spirit that day, yet I felt no different.

Did I miss something? Was I supposed to turn three times and click my heels at the end? I didn't understand that being filled with the Spirit of God wasn't a feeling, but a gift to receive. Feelings change. God is constant, the same yesterday, today and forever. And, before bed that night, I noticed the dull ache in my heart beginning to subside. I had a God-shaped hole in my heart that could only be filled by Him and that evening it was full!

As Michelle continued to meet with me, she soon discovered I didn't understand the character of God at all. Not only that, but I did not know what it meant to have my identity in Christ. I was unaware of the promises that come along with being adopted into the Kingdom of God as a daughter. I identified as an orphan; abandoned and alone. One who was not acceptable as I was.

I forfeited my rights as a daughter of the King by having the wrong ideas about God. I inadvertently negated the power of the blood shed for me at the cross when Jesus died for my shortcomings and disastrous choices. I strived for God's approval and believed nothing I ever did was good enough. The truth was, it would never be. But that is why I need Jesus. Because, even on my best day, I am still not sinless.

I was wrapped up in a web of lies I believed about myself and misinformation about God. I was defeated, and it was clear by the words that came pouring out of my mouth. The Word says, "...for out of the abundance of the heart his mouth speaks" (Luke 6:45 ESV). According to God, the heart really matters, and my heart was bitter, angry, and confused.

After listening to me, Michelle asked if I would be interested in coming to her house once a week for a play date while we learned some things about who Holy Spirit is. She was willing to take time with me, and I would not let this opportunity pass me by. Once again, God set up this beautiful relationship! Ruby spent her precious time teaching me about Jesus and now I would have Michelle to pick up the baton and run with me. This was God's beautifully appointed second checkpoint on assignment to teach me about Holy Spirit at an intimate level. Little did I know these meetings would radically transform me. All I knew was I hungered for more. For something different. For what she had that I did not.

IDENTITY

We spent that first time together discussing perceived identity vs. true identity. Even though there were times I was uncomfortable talking about things I didn't understand, I was drawn to the information. I wanted to know who I was in Christ and allow the power of the Holy Spirit to operate on the inside of me. I wanted to belong and rest in the peace that came with being labeled His.

Something I learned in all of those years of leadership training was that people and circumstances will try to place labels on you and it's up to us to either accept or reject those labels. We also have the power to label others. One of the most powerful stories related to this concept is that of a mother who empowered her labeled son.

In 1854, 7-year-old Thomas Edison came home from school one day with a letter from his teacher addressed to his mother. "Your son is addled [mentally ill]. We will not allow him to attend our institution any longer."

Her eyes blurred with tears as she read the letter to herself. But she did not accept what was written, nor would she allow Edison to believe them. Edison's mother told him the letter she received described how he was too smart for their school and he would be better taught at home. She prepared a homeschooling routine for her son and Edison left his school behind without a second thought.

After Edison's mother passed away many years later, he began the tedious task of going through all of his mother's earthly possessions. Sifting through old family records one day, Edison came across a letter buried deep in his mother's old closet. It was the letter from his elementary school that Edison's mother received many years before.

This passage would later be found in Edison's diary: "Thomas Alva Edison was an addled child, that, thanks to the heroism of his mother, became the genius of the century."[2]

Not only did this heroic mother not label her son mentally ill, but she also wouldn't let him know someone else had. She gave her son her own label. One that built him up as opposed to tearing him down. One that would allow her son to believe he really could achieve anything he wanted without limiting beliefs or false labels. After hearing this story, Nancy Edison became one of my greatest heroes, and I vowed to do for my children exactly what that mother did for her son.

Obviously, the time in history in which we live makes it more difficult to hide from the labels all around us. I was determined to teach my children not only that they existed, but how to handle them. I encouraged them to always consider the source and to never accept false labels. I taught them they had the power to accept or reject it. I wanted them to know they could do anything they wanted in life, to dream big and believe they would succeed. I never wanted flippant words from a teacher or one mistake to define my children.

Even though I taught this to them, it was so hard for me to grasp for myself. No one had to tell me I wasn't good enough. I believed that lie since I was a little girl. No words had to be spoken. I let life circumstances label me along with everything that left me feeling less than.

I wasn't pretty because I was overweight.

I wasn't smart because I struggled to remember things.

I wasn't worth much since no one protected me.

I believed I was no better than a dirty rag: used up, ugly, and useless. I believed I was worthy of nothing more than the life of abuse I lived. I accepted the lies spoken over me. "You should be grateful I take care of you. Consider yourself lucky. Without me you'd be in the street somewhere."

Abuse, abandonment, anger, rejection and fear all worked together to build an impenetrable fortress of bitterness and pain on the inside. For so long, I swept things under the rug and tried to pretend they didn't happen. Well, now my rug was bulging. There was no walking over it without tripping anymore. With Michelle's help, it was time to clean house.

We began a journey of healing my mind and emotions. This was no quick therapy session with a psychiatrist, where I took a little blue pill to fix everything. This was the beginning of my healing journey that would take nearly a decade to accomplish. Talk about intense spring cleaning!

We live in a world full of identity confusion. I've read articles about groups of people who identify as cats. There are even some who call themselves otherkins, identifying as mythical creatures and not as a human at all. Some may shake their head in complete disbelief at this, wondering how one might really believe they are a cat or a unicorn. But to be honest, most of us are living the same way.

We were created to be God's children. Though sin separated us from our Father, His heart toward us is the same. He sent His Son, Jesus, to Earth to live among us and teach us of His unfailing love. He shed His blood as a sacrifice for the sin of all mankind so that anyone who believes in Him would not perish in death, but live forever with God our Father. (John 3:15-18) By this great act of love, He showed all of humanity WHO we are to Him. We are valuable.

"What marvelous love the Father has extended to us! Just look at it—we're called children of God! That's who we really are. But that's also why the world doesn't recognize us or take us seriously, because it has no idea who he is or what he's up to." (1 John 3:1 MSG)

When we don't know who we are at our core, it's only because we don't know whose we are and to what family we belong. Often we don't recognize our true worth because we do not fully know the heart of God for us and His true nature and character. My view of God and myself was seen through the lens of past hurt, abuse, and neglect. I didn't trust Him at all. I believed He was disappointed in me for not being better, stronger, smarter, prettier, tainted by abuse and addiction and all the mistakes I'd made. I believed I was only one bad choice away from being cast out and left.

This couldn't have been further from the truth, and I was about to embark into uncharted territory to discover the truth and uncover the lies. The journey would be intense at times, and I wanted to give up because the pain seemed unbearable, but it's one I am eternally grateful for. Because one woman took her eyes off of her own comforts, opened her door to me, spent her precious mommy time with me while her little ones napped, and poured truth, love and acceptance into me, my life was changed. Her afternoon labor of love was a little like walking into a very cluttered and unorganized house filled with dust and cobwebs needing to be cleaned out. This was the first step in uncovering what was hidden beneath.

FORGIVENESS

Michelle sacrificed countless hours of her life to disciple me into wholeness. God knew I needed to do it this way, and He found a willing teacher. She began by helping me recognize all those false identities so that I could replace them with the truth of God and what He says about me. She helped me learn the danger of the unforgiveness I'd held in my heart and what it truly looked like to forgive.

I not only had to forgive my abusers, but myself as well. I needed to be set free from the chains that bound my future because of things that happened in the past. Being sexually abused, losing relationship with my mother, being homeless and walking into an abusive relationship at seventeen, all had pain attached and with that pain came unforgiveness.

As a judge would do, I was holding myself and others guilty. Unfortunately, I was not a fair judge, condemning harshly without mercy. I had taken the seat of the only true judge, Father God. I soon discovered that was not my job, and it wasn't up to me. What freedom this one revelation brought to my life! I could forgive and trust that God was just (Matthew 7:1-2, 2 Corinthians 5:10). With God's grace, I learned to release the need to condemn people I had no right to condemn. If He truly was good and He is, then I could trust Him with that.

He forgave me of all my past sins and brought me into his family. He didn't cast me out and leave me in the wilderness to die like I hoped would happen to my offenders. I had been forgiven of so much, not only in deed, but in thought. Jesus says, "Do not judge, and you will not be judged. Do not condemn, and you will not be condemned. Forgive, and you will be forgiven" (Luke 6:37 NIV). Jesus also gives us a warning about forgiveness that is not to be taken lightly; "If you forgive those who sin against you, your heavenly Father will forgive you. But if you refuse to forgive others, your Father will not forgive your sins" (Matthew 6:14-15 NLT).

It was clear I needed to let go of this dangerous unforgiveness. But how could I forgive a man who took my purity as a helpless three-year-old? How could I forgive someone who abandoned me? How about the ones who were unfaithful, abusive, or cruel? I thought forgiveness meant saying it was okay to hurt me and it's okay to do it again. To me, it looked like being a doormat for whoever wanted to wipe their muddy feet on. I believed forgiveness was impossible. I was in pain and that pain would not go away because I forgave. The overly used phrase, "forgive and forget," is not exactly a fair one to try to pass off as possible. Forgiveness doesn't erase the memories of pain, only Jesus can do that.

There didn't seem to be justice in forgiving. I believed if I forgave, then I let the offender off the hook. How would I ever make them pay for what they did to me if I forgave them? However, I learned forgiveness is not for the offender; it is for me. Forgiveness is releasing the grip that anger has on my heart. No matter how much I felt like I had a right to my unforgiveness, Jesus was clear in The Parable of the Unforgiving Servant that I do not (Matthew 18:21-35)!

Please understand, forgiveness is a process. You may read this right now, thinking, "You have no idea what's been done to me." I get it, really! Saying you should forgive and actually doing it are two very different things. I could not possibly have done it on my own or all at once. I couldn't forgive my current abuser at this point. As I later learned, it is a very difficult process to forgive a repeat offender.

I started the process of forgiveness by looking at the things that were no longer happening daily. I began with forgiving the man I called dad growing up. He had long passed away, and I hadn't seen or spoken to him in over fifteen years. How could I hold a dead man accountable? I needed to release my hatred.

Not knowing how to begin the forgiveness process was a large part of the reason I wasn't doing it. Michelle began teaching me this valuable practice by encouraging me to quiet my mind and focus on Jesus. Sitting on her overstuffed loveseat with a blanket across her lap, she said, "Ask God where He wants to heal you right now." As I sat in the quiet stillness of her living room and breathed, something shocking happened. I realized I was angry at Him first. This repressed anger toward God came rushing to the forefront.

In my mind, I stood in front of Jesus. He was close enough to touch. However, with a scowl on my face, I backed up. I was wearing filthy clothes filled with holes, tattered, and falling off of me. I glared at him with messy hair and hands that were balled into fists. I was an abandoned little orphan girl. Swirling around me and causing a barrier between us was my pain, and I directed it at Him. How could He have let me go through that? Why didn't He stop it? What kind of good and loving Father would have done nothing when someone was hurting His little girl? He left me!

The feeling of betrayal was overwhelming. A lump began forming in my throat and hot tears started flowing down my cheeks. Something inside was releasing. Until this point in my life, I didn't fully trust God. He showed me this was a big reason why. I wasn't expecting this to be what I would face when I asked the question.

Even though I was raging with anger toward Him, His face was so full of love and compassion. His demeanor demonstrated gentle patience. I asked Him why... why hadn't He stopped it?

Jesus then kneeled to my eye level, took my balled-up fists in His hands and grievingly apologized for what had happened to me. He wished it wasn't so. He assured me He was right by my side the entire time. As He spoke, the distance between us grew smaller and with every word, something changed in my heart. I was softening.

He then told me He had new clothes for me. Excitement welled up inside because anyone who knows me well knows I love getting new clothes! As I stood in His presence, He approached me in my broken state with dirt-streaked tears on my face. This time I stayed still and allowed Him to draw nearer. My eyes fixed on His, slowly He approached with a garment laid over his arms. With every step He took, He spoke a new word to me. Daughter. Loved. Precious. Clean. Pure. Mine.

He kneeled again, removing the tattered clothing from my little body, and replaced them with a stunning opal robe with a rich, purple border. His loving eyes remained fixed on mine. He wiped my face and brushed my messy hair and with each stroke I heard Him say without words, "I love you," over and over again.

All the unclean feelings I had from sexual abuse were being made clean in the presence of Jesus. He assured me it wasn't my fault. I hadn't caused that to happen to me. What a relief that was! I had felt the weight of that thought for as long as I could remember. I then allowed Jesus to show me where He was amid all that abuse.

He took me back to one time in particular when the man I called dad told me we were going for a ride to the creek in the middle of the afternoon. It terrified me to leave with him, but I had no choice. I knew what was going to happen. The only time we spent together was for his own perverted pleasure. As the memory came rushing in, so did the feeling of helplessness along with the anger at myself for not telling someone! This memory was different from some of the others. As we arrived at the dead-end gravel road where he would force me to get in the back of the blue Ford truck bed, I remember being so panicked but then nothing. I knew what was going to happen, but I don't remember what did.

While with Jesus, as the memory faded away, I asked, "Where were you Lord?" and immediately He showed me how He had taken me away during that dreadful event. We were in a field of delicate yellow and white flowers unlike any I've ever seen. We were just lying there looking up at the clouds and laughing together. There was only peace and simple joy in that moment.

I was undone! How loving He was. He had replaced the bad memory with a good one and just like that, it was gone. God healed me from the pain of that moment. The lie that I was helpless and abandoned had been replaced with the truth that He was always with me.

After cleaning up just a corner of the proverbial closet of my heart, I could begin the journey of learning who I really was. This release of pain allowed room for me to start accepting truth. I emptied myself of resentment and asked God to fill the places in me that only He could.

THE CHANGE

Michelle shared about the Holy Spirit, being baptized in the Spirit and the gifts associated with that. One such gift was that of speaking in tongues (1 Corinthians 12:8-10).

Growing up, I had not been taught the gifts of the Spirit and was told speaking in tongues was "of the devil", so my initial response was one of resistance. However, I was still drawn to this. I wanted all God offered. I knew what I had been doing so far wasn't working. I needed God to show me how to pray. I wanted desperately to know how to utilize all the weaponry I had access to so that I could protect myself and fight.

Even though I was skeptical at first, it didn't take me longer than five minutes of asking questions to realize this was not "of the devil" and I had to let Him do a great work in me. Either I was willing to do something different and change, or I could continue in my stubbornness, believing I knew what was best. I could choose to humble myself, become more teachable, and let true transformative change take place within my soul. I chose the latter!

Unfortunately, the closer I got to God and started to change inwardly, the worse things got at home. My confidence was growing as a daughter of the King as I uncovered who I was in Christ. I wanted Jerry to experience this with me and yearned for a loving relationship that was centered in Christ. I often voiced my desire to have this togetherness with him as a way of connecting. He was not interested. He believed this God stuff was a ploy to control him and point out all he was doing wrong. Asking for him to attend a church service with us or consider a marital counseling session or bible study was viewed as an attempt to ambush, change, and control. The resistance was intense. My desire to grow was viewed as an attempt to make him look bad.

His response was predictable, "You can stop trying to change me. I'm not the one with the problems. You are."

I tried to invite him into this amazing world of healing with me, but there was no going for him. He said he didn't need help, only crazy people needed counseling. I knew that wasn't true. If anything, the opposite was. Only crazy people refuse help and the opportunity to grow. I needed help, and I knew it. I wanted change so badly I was willing to throw off my pride that said, "I don't need this" and run as fast as I could into the unknown.

Same isn't always a bad thing, it can be a good thing too. Same is familiar and comfortable. However, it's when "same" causes us to completely resist change for the better that it becomes bad. I wanted to be open to what God wanted to change in my life. The things that didn't look like Him needed to go. The thoughts that were holding me in bondage and causing me to be a slave to the familiar had to go. I knew there were actions and addictions in my life that needed to change. The way I had been doing things was not working anymore, and I invited the shift.

It was hard then, and it still is. We are creatures of habit. I must fight myself often to make room for what God wants me to adjust. The change isn't so God can control us, but it's for our own benefit. I wanted Him to search my heart and pull out what was causing the rot in my soul (Psalm 139:23-24).

The heat intensified as I grew into who I was as a daughter of God and into a woman. When I met Jerry, I was young, scared, vulnerable, and alone. Now that I was becoming a new creation in Christ, I had a new boldness. I stood up for the things I knew were right when before, I would sit silent. He was losing the control he once had over me.

I can't tell you that seeking God, finding Him, and learning who I was created to be as His child made life easier. If anything, it made my life a lot more difficult at home. The friction was greater than ever before. My new confidence caused me to fight back when I needed to. Instead of letting Jerry run all over me with his words and push me around, I stood up for myself.

Change is hard! When change is met with resistance, our initial response is to want to quit and go back to what seemed easier. But familiar isn't always easier, it's just what we're used to. To remind myself that this change was good for me, I'd think back to the days before I knew who I was in Christ.

I knew I couldn't change Jerry, only he could decide that. However, I also knew that I could no longer stay silent about the things going on around me in my home. Any time I spoke up or resisted, it was met with name calling. Remember those false labels we talked about earlier? Those names he called me, even though I knew were untrue, still hurt and made me doubt myself.

I had a "you can't touch me" attitude on the outside, but on the inside, I still needed work to believe I was really who God said I was. I was being built up in my time with Jesus, only to be torn down by my husband. After listening to the bad things he'd say about me, I would wonder if those were true.

Maybe they were, who knows? God knew! So, I would crawl into the Lord's presence, beaten down and battered, asking Him the same question every time. "God, this is what Jerry said about me today. What do you say? Who do you say I am?" He'd pick me up off the ground, dust me off and remind me who I was time and time again.

I didn't have someone to call during those times I felt defeated. Normally, it was midnight before I could even get away from Jerry, so I only had two options. Either I went to sleep with those lies and waited until the next day to call a friend who would only empathize and try to encourage me. Or I could go straight to Father God about the events of the day and get it dealt with for good.

I found no real fulfillment in the "Power of Positive Thinking" type phrases I would post all over my bathroom mirror. "You can do it" seemed a little mocking, as a matter of fact. Those words were empty. I didn't believe them. I needed specific words to encourage me in WHO I was created to be and HOW God saw me. That was the only truth that penetrated the lies. His Words were the only ones that truly built me up and strengthened me for the next battle. All the other words were nice sayings, but they had no meaning without the foundation of God's breath speaking them to me first.

Old mindsets are difficult to break out of. The only way I could do it was to focus on allowing God to heal my heart and to pursue Him more than anything. The key to moving ahead was having someone to encourage me to keep going when things got too tough. Michelle was that person for me. She was a friend and mentor, but more than that, she had become my spiritual mother. She helped me grow, gave me guidance and a new perspective on life! I called on her when I needed a shoulder to cry on or to share about life over a warm cup of coffee. But, most importantly, when I struggled to believe I was who He said I was, she gently reminded me.

11

THE ULTIMATUM

I couldn't have continued my journey of discovering who I was in Christ without checkpoint people to encourage me each step of the way. Life is a marathon, not a sprint. When preparing to run a marathon, we must train. We need a coach to guide us in making healthy food choices, what gear to use, and how to recover correctly after each challenging workout. Just like a well-trained runner, I needed to have the right training from a coach who had experience. I had to replace the empty calories with fuel that would sustain me, such as the Word of God, prayer and praise. I needed someone to teach me to recover after being punched around in the boxing ring of life. I couldn't do it alone anymore. I just need to take a praise-cation right here and thank God for relationship! Thank you, God, for the amazing people you have placed and continue to place in my life. You are AWESOME!

No matter how well trained and prepared for the marathon set before you, there are inevitably unexpected obstacles on the journey. Maybe a pothole to avoid or a large rock you must jump over…then there are the huge gaping chasms somehow placed directly between you and where you're trying to go. They don't give warning of their arrival; they just show up.

For almost a year, things were going well as I progressed in my growth and understanding of who I was. I purposed to focus on my relationship with God and continued to gain a better understanding of His love for me. I began focusing less on the things I couldn't control and spent my days enjoying my children and pouring the new things I was learning for myself into them.

I continued to hope things would get better. I wondered when God would push a magic button that would change my home life and fix my spouse. I waited expectantly for Jerry to come around and decide to be a participant in life with us. I often thought that maybe he would see what God was doing and want to jump in. I learned to stay away from pointing out the things he did which hurt my heart or made me feel neglected. This never ended well, so I confronted him as little as possible. I wanted to keep the peace while I waited.

Life quickly went back to normal for Jerry after that terrible night of violence. The promises made to get back in the door were quickly forgotten. It was worse now than ever before. Even though he hadn't physically abused me, the emotional and verbal abuse had intensified.

I enrolled myself in college to pursue a nursing degree. It was becoming clear that I needed to find a way to set myself up for the future so I could provide for the children on my own. Each evening, after putting them to bed, I retreated to the basement to work on my studies and soak in His presence. I did this so I wouldn't have to hear him shouting curse words and obscene, dirty jokes at his teammates in the living room. The blaring machine guns and screaming were more than I could handle, and I knew what would happen if I got in his way.

He played games every evening, and the entire day he was off work. If we stayed home on his off days, we had no choice but to hear him. We were invisible, unless we got in his way. Unfortunately, it wasn't just for a couple of hours. There were many occasions he didn't sleep for days, so he could play. He'd only stop to eat, go to the bathroom and smoke. Most times, he didn't even stop to smoke. He took his controller outside with headset attached, lit up and stared through the window, continuing the game. I couldn't help but be embarrassed, wondering what the neighbors must think watching this full-grown man outside yelling through the window.

Eating meals, bathing the children, household chores and even sleeping were a daily challenge. Trying to live around this and ignore an open space in our home filled with rage and screaming obscenities was very hard. Honestly, as I write this today, I still hear the gunfire and cursing. It's crazy how memories can be so vivid after so many years.

This was a very hard time for me as a mother. Not only didn't I want to hear all this going on, but I also didn't want this environment for our children. At every opportunity, the children and I left for as long as possible. Occasionally, I would fight to get his attention for the kids' sake. See them, notice them… speak to them! My attempts would usually end defeated in tears. Even though I wanted him to pay attention to the children, it was usually best he didn't. He would say mean and hurtful things to our son that would break my heart. I had to step in and protect their hearts from his cruel words on many occasions. I felt powerless to stop the rage filled times. So, I tried keeping them out of his way as much as possible.

I compared this type of abuse to the abuse I witnessed growing up. Because it wasn't as bad, I figured it was something I just had to tolerate. I thought abuse had a sliding scale. No, the truth is abuse is abuse, period. It doesn't have a level of acceptability. Unfortunately, I hadn't realized that yet. Even though I knew that these were not healthy things for the children to endure, I didn't know what else to do about it.

Then, one day... enough was enough.

The day came when the line I didn't know existed had been crossed. For so long, I didn't know where my limit was; then all at once I did. I didn't understand what boundaries were or how to set healthy ones, yet somehow, I knew this was the edge of one. As a mother, I am called to protect my children against bodily and emotional harm. I was done just shuffling them out of sight to protect them. I couldn't just stand by and let this happen any longer. Suddenly, I no longer gave a reason or excuse to turn the other cheek. In this moment, on this day, I didn't care if I lived on the street. I just knew I couldn't allow what was taking place in the home to go on any longer.

The children and I were having dinner one evening in the dining room that was right off the living room. Jerry was sitting on the couch playing his video game as usual. Like most children, our son didn't want to eat his vegetables. David was the most compliant child 99% of the time. The 1% he wasn't always had to do with eating. It was an impossible fight with this stubborn, seven-year-old. Any moms out there feel my pain in this? Well, as most of us also know, if you're tired or having a rough day, little things can become big things quickly.

This particular evening, he stood his ground on the vegetable protest. Corn was the weapon, and I became the enemy. My tactic to get him to eat just one bite was to bribe him with dessert. If that didn't work, I would make him sit at the table until he did. I've since learned there are battles to be fought and then there are those you just surrender to because they aren't really that important. I gave him vitamins that had more nutrients than that canned corn. However, at this time, I still believed I was a terrible mom if my kids didn't eat vegetables. So, the battle ensued.

Children know that crying works when all else fails. His counterattack began, and the tears started as I continued to encourage him to take just one little bite! I was determined to have victory! He finally relented by putting a few kernels of corn in his mouth. He immediately heaved as though he was going to throw up. There didn't seem to be any hope that I could win this battle and I couldn't stand to see him suffer so much at the hand of corn. It wasn't funny then but; I chuckle now because to this day my now eighteen-year-old refuses to eat vegetables of any kind.

I was just about to give in and let him leave the table to get ready for bed when we awoke to the sleeping dragon. As the video game controller went flying across the living room, I knew what was coming and prepared to protect our son. Jerry stomped into the dining room, grabbed David's little arm, yanked him out of his chair, and began shoving him towards the stairway. He was shouting and calling him degrading names. After kneeing him in the tailbone, he screamed for him to go to his room.

I quickly picked up our daughter to keep her from being injured in the crossfire and jumped between Jerry and David. Pleading with him to stop, I shuffled the children up the stairs, trying to keep his attention on me and off them. I stood at the bottom of the stairs as they scrambled up and firmly declared to him he was not getting by me. He put his forehead on mine and pressed it into me. With all the terror he could muster, he screamed at me to get out of his way.

I stood my ground, hoping he wouldn't push me down and go, anyway. I firmly responded, "No, I will take care of them. Don't worry about it. I got them. Just go back to your game and we'll be quiet."

After a battle of intense staring to see who would budge first, he gave in and went back to his game. But not without flinging a couple choice words my way. This rage was a gross overreaction to the situation. His violence increased for each encounter and was significantly worse if we interrupted his gaming. What started as a normal evening ended up atomic.

I held my children as they cried, obviously scared and upset about what had just occurred. We talked about it as I tried making excuses to them about why daddy acts the way he does and assured them it was not their fault. I apologized for everything that happened. We talked, played, and read stories until bedtime. After getting the children to sleep, I thought maybe enough time had passed and I could have a conversation with Jerry. I needed to address how unreasonable and out of control his behavior was.

I knew from experience that reasoning with someone who doesn't see things from a reasonable perspective doesn't end well, but I went in anyway. I began by asking him if we could talk and if he would mind putting the controller down for just a few minutes. With no response, I should have walked away but instead began talking to this brick wall that sat on the couch across from me. He wouldn't even acknowledge me, staring straight ahead at the TV with the controller in hand.

I'm hardheaded sometimes and I'd had enough. I explained to Jerry that life could not keep going on like this. The way he treated the children, and I had to change. He continued to ignore me, except for his occasional famous words, "Whatever, Kathryn."

I could tell I was getting nowhere, but I desperately wanted him to hear my heart! After trying to talk to him with no response, as a last resort ditch effort, the ultimatum came out. Either put the video game down and quit playing or the kids and I were leaving. I did not know where we would go, with no money and the closest family more than a thousand miles away. I said it before I really thought it through. These words came out easily though, because they'd been in my heart for a long time.

Once those words came out of my mouth, they were met with prideful anger. Cursing me, he said, "Go ahead and leave. You're never going to make me quit playing my game."

I was both devastated and relieved all at the same time. I was torn. My heart wanted us to be a normal family. I'd invested years of prayer for him and our relationship to improve. I'd spent many nights studying what it meant to lay down my soul for my spouse and forgive. I spent countless hours hoping change would one day show up at my doorstep.

Instead, I faced a resounding NO. Things would not change, and I needed to move on. It's not that God didn't answer my prayers for change. Change was happening even if it wasn't in the way I imagined. It was happening in me. I was becoming less tolerant of the mistreatment and abuse and more confident that God wanted better for me and I was worthy of it. God will not force anyone to change. We are given the gift to choose our path. I wouldn't be the one to make Jerry change. He had to want that for himself. There needed to be a separation, and I was ready to face the challenges that came with it.

The financial challenge would be the greatest. I was painfully aware I would have to support two children on my own. He had other children he never paid child support for with no consequence. I had no doubt I'd be in the same position. I was on my own.

Even though there was a lack of finances, I started looking at what I could do instead of focusing on what I couldn't. That night I stayed up well into the early morning, planning my next moves and the timing. I would present the idea to him that I would need two weeks to pack, get an apartment, and get out.

Thankfully, I took my grandmother's advice and put away a little money as often as I could. It wasn't much, but it was a start. It wouldn't be enough for the first month's rent and deposit anywhere, but I could have that in a couple of weeks. I'd decided I didn't need more than a one-bedroom apartment. I didn't care about comfort anymore. I wasn't planning on moving far. I just wanted to be in a safe environment with my kids and to live peacefully.

However, the very next morning, as I made my way to the coffeepot, Jerry proudly announced that there would be a U-Haul delivered by the end of the week and he was leaving me. He hadn't slept at all and was in a peculiar mood. During the night, he quit his job and was moving back to Kentucky. It felt as if he were spitting in my face. As if to say, I'm about to make you regret your life. He was delighting in my panic as I was suddenly aware he was leaving me with a huge rental payment, all the bills, and no way out. Even though I had no idea how I would take care of it all, I was determined to stand tall and show no fear.

Things were difficult the rest of the week as words flew at me like daggers. I had to continuously clean up the confusion and explain what was happening to our children. When they asked him why he was leaving, his response was, "Your mother is kicking me out. Maybe you can come live with me soon since your mom won't be able to take care of you."

He used his words like a weapon to attempt to destroy me. They were his proverbial fists, both covered with brass knuckles.

The hardest part of all of this was the pain and confusion it brought to the children. To a child, a separation of parents is hard no matter what. However, I believe there are healthy ways to handle it and things that can be said to help the children try to understand. As parents, we have the power to make it better or worse for them. Seeing that I would be the only one thinking of their needs in this area, I kept trying to calm, reassure, and distract them as much as possible. I had to protect their hearts and minds. Prideful selfishness and flippant words flung around made an already difficult situation worse.

Instead of being able to sit down together with the kids and explain things in a way that they may understand, they were getting mixed messages they had to sort out. I made excuses for him where I could and tried to protect them from the way things were for so long, but there was nothing more I could do. There was no smoothing this over. I had to let him go in order to begin the clean-up process.

As much as I wanted to, I decided I couldn't stay in California. It was far too expensive. I'd only planned on staying before because I didn't want to prevent the children from seeing their dad. Now, he was leaving without concern for this very thing. Although my heart was broken as I saw all the changes I hoped for crumble before me, I had no choice but to put one foot in front of the other and seek to provide for the children. Realistically, I couldn't do it on the waitress income I was making alone. I needed a better job.

The first few days after he left were strangely peaceful, and the quiet was wonderful. I was grieving the loss of the hope for change I held onto for so long. I was also concerned about how to provide for the children while helping them understand why their daddy moved so far away. However, there was a calm I felt amid all the uncertainty.

I sought direction from God and asked Him to guide my next move. I reached out to my sister, Hannah, for comfort and to help me brainstorm. I couldn't stay in my home long. The rent was more than I made all month. Thankfully, she had some ideas. Her husband was in upper management and it just so happened that we used to work together at the same place. Therefore, he knew my work ethic, character, and abilities.

Once she shared my situation with him, it wasn't long before they presented a job to me to open a new store for his franchise. It appeared it would be a perfect fit! Although, it meant moving to a tiny town in Kentucky where I wouldn't know anyone and the closest family would be three hours away. It also meant I would have to give up finishing my college degree.

None of that mattered, though. I would be able to financially support my children and finally be free! For the first time in my life, I was excited about the future! I had peace inside as I prayed about the decision and asked God to confirm the move. As I walked up and down the main street on Google Maps, my heart leaped with joy when I saw all the beautiful trees in the little town.

Hannah flew to California to help me move. The plan was to stay with her during the summer while we waited for the store to finish being built. It was supposed to be on track for completion by August! Perfect timing to get the kids enrolled in school and start our new life. I was unafraid, independent and peaceful!

12

WHO MOVED MY DUCK?

The one thing in life that is constant is that there will always be change. We can make our plans, cross our T's, dot our I's, put all our ducks in a row and count our ducks. A day will come when the narrative changes and all our ducks fall off a cliff!

Soon after arriving at my sisters, I found out that the man I had just gained my freedom from was living two blocks away. Naturally, he thought I was there to be near him, when really, I wanted to be as far away as possible. I had no intention of staying; I was merely supposed to be there for two months while I worked to save money for a home to rent.

Jerry assumed I'd followed him and wanted to move back in together. I had no intention of this until I saw an actual change in his life. I was focusing on gaining independence from him. I needed to heal areas that were continually under attack. I couldn't do that with him around and the toxic environment he brought along.

When he arrived in Kentucky, while I was still in California with our children, he sought out my siblings and began weaving a web of lies that trapped those who heard it. He was a great wordsmith, and they listened to his woes of my insanity over the video game he played. To my surprise, once I arrived, not only wasn't anyone on the same page as me, no one was even in the same book.

From his perspective, the only issue we had was that I didn't like how much he played video games. I couldn't understand how, even after being crystal clear about the way the children and I were treated; he still didn't see that as a potential problem in our marriage. It seemed as if he believed I should accept his behavior without reproach.

I didn't share how I he treated me with everyone in my family. I wasn't interested in fighting to convince them to believe what I was living through when it didn't matter, anyway. God and I knew the truth, and that was enough. It was exhausting enough to deal with it without having to rehash every detail to everyone. However, Jerry wasted no time laying out his case like a lawyer to the jury. They didn't understand what my problem was, either.

Experience taught me to pick battles worth fighting, and it didn't matter to me if they were on his side or mine. I was tired of fighting and focused on the dream of a life of peace.

Waiting is hard. During this season, I was without a home of my own and relied solely on the support of others. I second guessed myself as a mother more during this time than ever. Huge boulders of negative criticism were hurled my way daily. My siblings reprimanded me for being overprotective of my children. "You care too much" was something I heard regularly when it came to what I let my children watch or listen to. Should I have cared less? No! I had to remind myself often that there was a war for their hearts and minds. I would not back down!

Parenting is also hard. Harder than I ever imagined possible, yet just as rewarding. How could I take what had been entrusted to me, throw caution to the wind, and forget the gravity of this responsibility? I had to do what I felt was the right thing, no matter the opposition.

During the wait, I often felt isolated for being different. But I knew that just because everyone else was doing something didn't make it right. I was determined to teach this to my children. I had to stand my ground in my convictions. The influence of the enemy would not be allowed to infiltrate my young, impressionable children's minds without a fight. I could not just shrug my shoulders and hope they learned on their own.

When I tried to explain my reasons behind protecting their eyes and ears, it only made my anxiety and stress levels higher. Eventually, I stopped voicing my hurt and trying to convince my family of my decisions. This was a losing battle. I was breaking under the weight of my loneliness. I needed Father God to cheer me on, but it was so hard to hear Him through all the noise and chaos.

Unfortunately, my sister's husband was Jerry's gaming buddy, and there was an "open-door" policy for him to come over anytime he wanted. This created so much tension for me and confusion for the children. I couldn't hide from him in the same house. Without fail, at some point during his stay, he would corner me into a conversation. It always started the same way; things will be different this time. However, when met with my "been there, done that" responses, his anger flared. He hadn't changed. He was the same person using the same tactics, and this time I was determined not to fall for it again.

I had a plan! Remember all those ducks I put in a row? I didn't need to believe his lies anymore because I could take care of myself. I no longer needed to take his bait. I was going to be free of all this pain. I kept looking forward to my next destination with blinders on. I focused on looking for a house to rent and planning the three-hour move. However, the closer we got to August, the more concerned I became. I wasn't so sure that I could do it alone after all.

I saw my tower of plans beginning to sway in the stormy wind brewing in the distance. I'd put all my hope in this one job to pave the way for me to make it on my own. I still didn't trust God enough to be my provider and take care of my needs. I trusted my abilities, and the weight of it all rested on my shoulders. By mid-July, construction on the stores building had yet to begin. I shoved away all my doubts and determined this would work out. After hearing that the promised construction would now be completed by late August, I decided to relocate to the area with my children.

I'd worn out my welcome at Hannah's house and tensions were high in the home. To save our relationship, it was time to move out, no matter what. I did not know which direction to go. If I stayed and waited for the building process to be completed, I would have to find a home to rent. This meant losing the money I'd saved for the move.

Afraid I'd miss out on the job, I saw no other choice but to move and get started with our new life in our new town. I hoped I'd find other work for a little while to keep me going while I waited. I was uncertain I was making the right decision, but I didn't know what else to do. I felt drawn to this little town where I knew no one so I took a leap into the unknown.

Once we got settled into our new place, I began the search for a temporary job. Weeks were going by and there were no signs of life at the construction site. My savings were dwindling, and I was getting more anxious every day. I reached out to see if there was any news on the construction timeline. Unfortunately, the response was the one I'd feared most. There would be no store built after all. There was a vote in the town meeting against allowing that particular franchise into the city. There was concern it would overshadow the local mom-and-pop shops. Apparently, this was the delay the entire time.

My heart sank and my stomach felt nauseous. I'd made a huge mistake and gotten myself into a mess! What was I thinking? I moved to a town where I didn't know anyone and now I had no job prospect. My desperation and lack of patience in the waiting once again caused me to overlook things, like having a secure job contract with the franchise owner before moving.

The negative self-talk began ramping up and survival mode kicked in. I gave in to the lie that I only had one choice left. I would have to go back to him. Word of my situation got to Jerry before I even fully decided I would call and ask him for help. Like a vulture, he circled, waiting to pick off whatever was left of me.

He called one day to offer me a deal, since he knew I was in a desperate situation. He was still living in a friend's house, rent- free, but he had a great job that paid well. He was determined to make sure I knew how much he made and that he was still not going to pay child-support if I ever took him to court. So, if I wanted help, this was his offer. Because of his living situation, he couldn't suggest we move in with him. Instead, he'd continue to stay where he was, work and give me money to cover our living expenses. But I had to…

As usual, there was a catch. As I held my breath, waiting for it to spew out of his mouth, I could hear my heartbeat in my ears. My stomach was in knots as I waited for "the deal". To receive his money to help me take care of our children while I looked for a job, I'd have to agree he could stay at my place every weekend. I knew this meant giving him back the control. His terms, his way… now his house.

I knew what he really wanted. My stomach tightened even more at the thought of having to give in to take care of our children. I had been so hurt and so tired of being used. I didn't want him near me, let alone in my house. This separation was supposed to be permanent. At least it was in my mind.

It had been over three months and, based on what I had already seen, I was certain change was not coming. I didn't want to be divorced again, but it seemed painfully clear this was the way it had to be. I had resolved this season was ending. I was ready to put behind me the constant reminders of unfaithfulness, anger, and abuse. I'd been captive to this life for too long and yearned to be free.

However, I had not yet filed for divorce. I didn't have any idea which direction to go to do that, nor did I have the finances necessary. Besides, I was terrified of making the first step. I was afraid of making the wrong decision. I'd been so conditioned to second guess myself that I had no self-confidence. The seeds that carried lies about who I was and what I was capable of had grown deep roots that could only be destroyed by truly trusting God as my provider and lover of my soul (Philippians 4:19, Psalm 23:3).

Intimidation and manipulation are the enemy's game (2 Corinthians 11:14, John 8:44). His strategy was to dominate with confusion, uncertainty, and fear, keeping me bound in this cycle. I often did what I felt was necessary to survive. I'd lived in survival mode most of my life, but this was not just about me anymore. I had to think about my children, too.

Because I had very little self-confidence, I bowed to fear. I was in a constant state of worry about the future and lack of provision. I learned that to have my physical needs met, I had to perform. What I received was contingent on what I did in return or what I allowed to go on without speaking up. I didn't know what it felt like to be cared for or loved without conditions.

True self-confidence is cultivated by knowing the character of God and believing that what He says about you is true. When we believe His promises are true, we can trust His Word. When we know how loved, supported and accepted we are, we can relax and trust that God has our best interest in mind and will take care of us. If we believe He is really a good Father, then doesn't a good Father take care of his children's needs? Aren't we His children (Matthew 7:11)?

Living with low self-confidence could've been canceled out if I had confidence in my Father. God-confidence is so much better. Even though I had no self-confidence, I could still be confident, knowing it wasn't up to me to make it work. I just needed to take a step and God would take care of the rest.

God-confidence is the medicine that heals the need to perform to be accepted. It's a knowing so deep within us that nothing and no one can convince us otherwise. I wasn't fully there yet.

I had head knowledge about God's character and promises, but not the heart knowledge. What I had learned about God so far was wonderful and I wanted to believe what He said was true, but I wasn't fully confident that it was for me. I had some major trust issues because I hadn't experienced this security in any relationship in my life. This made it hard to imagine what true security would look like.

I battled this deep-seated performance mentality, planted from childhood. To keep the peace and get what I needed with the least amount of resistance, I needed to be good and do what I was told.

Even though the work to remove this had begun inside of me, I was still under major construction. My construction site was noisy! Unfortunately, the loudest voice I heard was that of fear and intimidation.

The intimidation came in the form of threats and lies that often sounded like this: If you don't let me in, I won't help you with the children's needs. You'll be a bad mother for not taking care of them. I am your only way. I am your provider, remember... you are nothing without me. You can do nothing without me... you are nothing without me.

The little self-confidence I'd built in my new relationship with God wasn't enough to override those lies. Because I still hadn't learned to trust Him, I believed I had to rely on Jerry to survive. Reluctantly, I agreed to the proposal. After I hung up the phone that day, I cried until I felt I had no tears left in me. I immediately regretted my "yes", because I could almost hear the slamming of the prison door. Defeated, I walked back into my cell, found my old familiar corner and hunkered down for the long haul.

My mind was reeling with thoughts of frustration, disappointment, and anger. I was angry at myself for saying yes so quickly, for not being strong and coming up with another way. I knew this plan was his way of trapping me again, and I walked right into it. Angry and disgusted with myself, the next thought that came across the tape player of my mind was an old familiar one... I hate you for being weak.

I hoped I could find a job quickly and end "the deal". I continued my search and re-enrolled in college. After months of Jerry coming and going as he pleased, my peaceful haven, our fresh start, my home, became his again. He soon began bringing his Xbox with him so he could play the game that caused me so much physical and emotional pain. When I would protest, he reminded me of whose house I was living in with familiar words. "I pay these bills and if you don't like it, you can leave." Here we were again!

I had learned to function in my dysfunction. I learned how to function in the pain and accept the thought that this is just the way it was. I was terrified of living freely even though I wanted to. A greater part of me was uncertain how to act in the world without my victim mentality. The idea of living without the daily pain and heartbreak was one I couldn't quite imagine. All I had ever known was abuse and dysfunction. I adapted and learned to make it work. It was my normal. This was also part of the reason I stayed in an abusive, less than ideal situation. Even when I could have been free from it, I kept going back.

I can compare what I dealt with mentally to this example. Let's imagine for a moment I have a friend; we'll call her April. April was born with a birth defect and had no use of her arms or legs. As she grew, she relied on the full attention of both her parents to care for her every need. All their energy was focused on April. Her parents took her to some of the best doctors in the world to come up with a solution and cure for April's disability. Years passed and still no answers. She was told she would always rely on someone else for care.

April grew into a young woman. Her parents had given up hope she would ever be cured and often said things to reinforce that such as, "It's just the way it is, sweetie. We'll take care of you."

She had become a victim with no hope of ever being able to do anything for herself. One day, the phone rang. An institute heard of April's condition and was confident they could help. Her parents were skeptical but excited. When they presented the idea to April, she became angry, screaming at them to leave her alone. She was not interested in being healed. Her parents were shocked! What?! How could she not want to be healed? Why wasn't she even willing to try?

The truth was, April wanted to be healed but was used to relying on others to take care of her. She was terrified of the idea that if she got better, she would have to be 100% responsible for her own care. She feared no one would see her if she did not need help all the time. She didn't know how to live outside of the confines of her wheelchair.

Yes, she wanted to be like everyone else and live a normal life, but she had never done that. Would she be able to make it on her own? What if no one cared about her anymore because they weren't caring for her every need?

This was how I lived. Chained to my victim mentality and uncertain how to function without it. Even though I dreamed of what it might be like to live a normal life, I wasn't sure I could make it. I had been bound in the chains of lies and hopelessness so long, how could I live free? I became like April. Scared of taking a risk to be fully healed. I was okay with the idea of it, but when it came right down to actually stepping out, fear of the unknown kicked in and I stayed just the way I was.

The longer I stayed, the more distorted my vision became and the harder it was to see a way out. I kept choosing the familiar over the unknown to have protection and provision from Jerry. I'd determined that this was my fate.

A few short months later, Jerry got a new job in a nearby city and moved in full time with us again. I was still without full-time employment and there didn't seem to be any other way. There wasn't really a discussion about it. He just showed up one day with all his stuff and life would resume as it was before. I didn't have a choice. He paid most of our living expenses.

On top of the emotional and verbal abuse, I overlooked countless findings of unfaithfulness in my marriage. Mainly because

I couldn't prove Jerry had actually been unfaithful. The evidence alluded to it; the intentions were emailed, the dating site profiles were in place, but I wasn't sure if he ever followed through. When confronted, he used a tactic to confuse me with diversions, exhaustion, and words.

"I'm so sick of this crap," I complained. "It's always the same thing. Why do I put up with this? Why do I stay?" His rebuttal laced with indifference, "I don't care, Kathryn. Go ahead and leave. See how far you get," followed by mumbling something about me living in a ditch.

My which I would reply, "How can you not care at all? How would you feel if you found me doing the same things? How can you think this is okay to do?" Met with, "Do what Kathryn?" And round and round we'd go. Each time he'd weave a story so confusing that it left me unsure of which way was up or down.

Jerry went to church with us occasionally, but usually had an excuse for when he stayed away. "I just can't be like those people, Kathryn." But he didn't realize "those people" were just as broken. We all are, and we all need to be healed. And no matter how good we try to be, we all need Jesus. If we could be good enough on our own, then what did He die for? I believe church should be a place to come when we're broken, not wait until everything's perfect. Staying away because we're not in a place of perfection is like ignoring a broken foot when we need to go to the hospital.

Jerry often referenced scripture, but only when I brought up the idea of leaving because of the perceived infidelity. He reminded me of what the Bible says about divorce, usually ending with something like how I'd go to hell if I left, and God would never help me. What I had yet to realize was that, yes, God does hate divorce, but he also gives two stipulations where it's okay. One of those is infidelity (Matthew 19:9)! I am sure Jerry didn't know that, either.

If he was ever truly concerned, I might be serious about leaving, he'd pull out the guilt and manipulation cards and they worked every single time. Jerry tried to convince me he'd never actually slept with any of the women he messaged, so it wasn't cheating. I couldn't prove his physical unfaithfulness, but it felt the same to me. I reasoned with myself that I could pretend it didn't happen. After all, ignorance is bliss, right?

After listening to his excuses for so long, I felt like I was going crazy. I couldn't say for certain if he was telling the truth, although deep down I knew. Eventually, exhaustion set in because he wouldn't let me sleep until he felt confident I believed him. I didn't have the stamina to fight him. Exasperated, I gave into the lie that maybe it really was my fault, anyway.

As the months turned into years, I tried to keep our interactions to a minimum. If I could only keep my head down and focus on the children, my job, and my relationship with God, I reasoned I would be fine. I had a desire to live a whole, healed, and healthy life. With new wounds being formed every day and old scabs being ripped off, it seemed it would be a never-ending process.

Each time I gained a little strength, there'd be another battle waiting, leaving me winded and weak. I continued pushing away the whispers to give up. If I listened, I knew I would. I had to find a way to strengthen myself in the Lord.

While I naively waited again for change to come, my relationship with God grew. I needed Him to just take my next breath each time I found evidence of infidelity. Without God, I would crumble at the next insult. In the waiting, I ran to God instead of away from Him when things got tough, which meant I was running to God constantly. Although I wasn't sure if my circumstances would ever change, I had to stop focusing on them and focus on healing so I would be stronger and better equipped to handle the attacks when they came. The pain of staying the same finally became greater than the pain of change.

Life had broken me, but I was too stubborn to stay broken. I didn't like what I saw in the mirror or who I was inside. Bitterness had taken up residence in my heart and anger guarded the door. I finally asked myself the hardest question I've ever had to answer,

"Who do you want to be?" Instead of being broken, I wanted to be whole. I knew to be healthy, both mentally and physically, my wounds needed to be healed. I don't know if I can pinpoint one exact moment when I made this decision to forge a new path. I believe it was a series of thoughts over the course of many years that led to this desire for more. There was a mighty warrior spirit within me that was ready to rise and do whatever it took. I just had to nourish it.

THERAPY

I've always loved writing and found it therapeutic when I was young. For a season, I stopped writing altogether because I was afraid it would be discovered and used against me. After hearing countless times about the power of journaling, I thought I better get back to it and hide the notebook if I had to. I found journaling to be the key in releasing pain and replacing lies with truth. This was where I could hear God the clearest. I was not always consistent, but every time I wrote, God showed up. Writing was my therapy; God was the therapist.

I needed to see the thoughts and feelings inside of me flood out onto the paper. The physical movement of the pen was necessary to focus on releasing the pain. This was my secret meeting place with God. A place I could hear Him speak through the noise. This was where the lies met truth. The words of truth and love from the

Father poured over me like a healing balm. Each time I wrote, I could see a definitive shift in the writing where it had switched from my words to Abba Father's.

Such healing occurred alone in my bedroom, with no one's shoulder to cry on but God's. I shut the door and wrote without the need to impress anyone. I could express myself without the fear of being made to feel like something was wrong with me. God could handle my anger, my ugly, and my pain. He could even handle my uncertainty about Him and His goodness. He didn't turn His back on me when I revealed how untrusting I was and why. He already knew and was ready to speak to me about all of it in the pages of my journal.

In the years I wrote on the pages in those journals, He wrote on the page of my heart. My relationship with God the Father continued to deepen as I learned more about Him and what His Word said about me. I knew to truly believe I was who He said I was in Christ. I had to trust Him.

I have often heard the quote that ignorance is bliss and what you don't know can't hurt you. I firmly disagree. What you don't know could actually kill you! If you were to drink bleach because no one had ever told you it was poison, would that be bliss? Of course not! Likewise, I needed to know what God's Word said. If I don't know what His instructions are, how can I follow them? If I don't know His character, how then can I trust Him? If I do not know what He says about me as His child, who then should tell me?

There was an increased urgency to know what God said about me and to know Him greater. I knew going to church once a week to be fed would not be enough. I couldn't starve during the week. I began by making small changes to grow. Instead of the radio, I listened to podcasts with sermons from pastors that encouraged me and taught me more about this God who loved me just as I was. I wrote out scripture from the Word, taping 3x5 index cards all over my bathroom mirror, refrigerator, and even on the dashboard of my car. They weren't Pinterest perfect wall posters or pretty stickers from Etsy, but they were powerful reminders of His promises in my darkest moments.

Without God, I saw no hope for my future. I could not rely on my own strength or anyone else to pick up the pieces of my shattered heart. Only God could do it. When I was the most broken, He came to my rescue. The storms of this life left me tattered and torn, like a sail that had been ripped from its mast. I was being tossed to and fro in the wind until He reached out and grabbed hold of me. I wasn't dismissed as garbage because I was broken. He took what was dirty and washed it. What was broken, He began to mend. The great craftsman saw potential in my life. I was becoming part of a new purpose (Psalm 34:18).

13

UNCHARTED TERRITORY

I stood staring at the dense jungle ahead, no path in sight. It would be hard, tiring, and at times lonely, but it had to be done. I had a destination to get to. Healing was waiting on the other side! I was ready to forge a path.

With the Word of God, my machete in one hand and Holy Spirit, a torch of fire to light the way, blazing in the other, I charged into the unknown. The cry of my heart, "It starts and ends with me," was a constant reminder to myself that I was going to be the generation of change. My children would know a different way of life. I charged ahead into the wild brush, not knowing which direction to go. I had to listen and take time to stop and rest when needed if I wanted to get to where I was going safely.

Forging a new path in a dense jungle can be a daunting task. Sometimes exhaustion or loneliness set in and I felt I couldn't go on.

Instead of listening and seeking the next step, I'd set up camp and stay in one place for long periods of time while coddling my victim mentality and licking my wounds after an attack. When I finally decided to keep moving forward, I would initially wonder if God had left me because I camped out too long.

To my surprise, He was right there waiting for me every time. He never left me as I wallowed in my sorrow when things were too hard. He stopped with me, waited, and lovingly encouraged me to get up.

At the beginning of my healing journey, I understood so little about God and His kingdom order. In His gracious way, He poured out understanding in small doses so I wouldn't get overwhelmed and patiently called my name down the path I was trudging so I wouldn't get lost. Many times, I could have unknowingly taken one step to my left and fallen off the edge of a cliff to the sharp rocks below. The brush was so thick I wouldn't have known it. There was so much I couldn't see.

When I chose not to listen to His voice, I stumbled as I moved forward. But I got back up each time and listened again with more intention, avoiding the trap the enemy was laying in the path unseen.

Hard things still occurred in my life, but I was able to keep my footing. Even though I didn't fully trust God yet, I wanted to. I wasn't sure of Him. I didn't know if He would leave me from one moment to the next. I went back and forth with myself, trying to accept that He was a good Father and had my best interest in mind. He was my only option, and I was willing to take the risk to find out.

I believe the decision to learn how to trust Him and be obedient saved me from so much more pain and suffering. Life can be much like walking a minefield. God sees what we can't. He gave me the map to get to the other side with all my limbs attached, but the catch was I had to follow it to stay in one piece and arrive on the other side as quickly as possible.

The way God works leaves me in awe. He collects pieces of our life that appear to be insignificant at a glance and works them together to form a beautiful masterpiece. When we discredit a piece of our lives as unimportant, He sees where it fits into the finished product. Without it, the result wouldn't be the same! We can't see the big picture while we are moving ahead. It's not until we look back that we can see the pieces being woven together and gain clarity to see that He really does work all things out for our good and His Glory (Jeremiah 29:11).

A couple of years prior to moving back to Kentucky, as I was driving my littles to the park, I heard God speak. It came out of nowhere, and like every other time, made no sense. He simply said, "You will work for my church."

My response was immediate, "What? I don't think so. Only

pastors work for churches, and I am going to be a nurse."

This word from God met with my response of, "Yea, right!" would take years to come to pass. This wasn't even a desire of my heart. My life was such a mess. How could I work for a church? Didn't God know how messed up I was?

I often responded to God this way. I heard a direction, or He would give me a vision for my life, and I questioned His every word. However, instead of asking out of curiosity, it was because I didn't trust God. I was defensive and uncertain He had my best interests in mind.

I wanted to know the entire picture so I could decide if it would be okay with me. I usually had a plan and felt He should jump on board with my ideas, not the other way around. I was unwilling to release the steering wheel of life and allow God to guide me. I hadn't learned yet that God is sovereign and if I would release control to Him, I would be taken care of.

It was painfully clear that I needed to find community with those who would encourage and pray for me. This was the only way I could survive and move forward. What better place to start than in church? Even though I still struggled with feeling like I didn't fit in, I pushed past that familiar voice, telling me to stay home. Whether I wanted to go or not, I had to get away from my environment... physically and mentally. Surrounding myself with encouraging people was vital. In exchange, I could deal with being uncomfortable in the process.

I'd only been attending church in my new town for a couple of months when they announced they needed help sorting clothes for an upcoming outreach. I thought, I can sort clothes, I love clothes. Since I still wasn't working, I had free time, so I went to help!

The day for organizing came. I enjoyed being with the other women and feeling useful. After we finished this task, we put up a Christmas tree in the foyer and cleaned the office space. While the remaining ladies were busying themselves with other things that needed done, the pastor's wife, Amy, and I hung ornaments.

As we worked, I couldn't help but feel like I was being interviewed on a talk show. She had so many questions. As soon as I answered one, she had another one waiting in the wing. I wasn't used to someone being so interested in me! I appreciated her genuine and sincere intrigue. Even if crafting the answers was uncomfortable, I felt comfortable with her.

When I left California and the support of my sisters and mothers in Christ, I prayed this prayer several times on the thirty-hour drive. "God, please bring me spiritual mothers to help me when I get there." Now here I stood talking to my answered prayer.

I knew it from the moment we first met for coffee. As I walked back to my car, I heard the Lord whisper, "Remember what you asked for?" and I immediately remembered my request just months earlier.

I was like a baton being passed to the next runner in the relay race of life, and Amy was receiving the baton. She was going to be the next in line to continue teaching me about the character of God. I would learn how to be a daughter and trust God as my Father. She showed what grace looks like. It would be through this relationship that I'd come to know the magnificent, endless love God has for me, just as I am. This was only one of many little glimpses to come that reinforced the truth that God truly sees me and provides everything I have need of. Both Amy and her husband Joseph paved the way for trust between God and I.

While adding the finishing touches to the Christmas tree, the focus of the conversation moved from my past to my future.

"We're looking for someone to help us at the office a couple of days a week," she began as I quietly listened.

My only response was, "Oh?!" not having a clue why she was sharing this need with me. I was new to the area and didn't know anyone to recommend and she certainty couldn't be thinking of asking me.

She continued, "Yes, and I've had a couple of people in mind to ask, but every time I bring those names to God, He puts your face in front of them."

Wait?! What? She can't be asking me to fill the position, could she? I'd only known her for three months and even then, we'd only had a couple of conversations. I wasn't even an official member of the church. She stopped fidgeting with the tree, looked me straight in the eye and asked, "Would you be interested in being our assistant and working here in the office?"

Standing there in complete shock, the words "You will work for my church someday," flooded my mind. These were the words God had spoken to me just a year and a half ago. But wait, God, how could I get offered a position I didn't apply for?

Fighting to compose myself and mask my shock, I responded. "Um, well, I don't know."

Insert long awkward silence. "Maybe?! Can I pray about it and get back to you?" The typical Christian answer when you want to get out of having to commit to something without being pushed. Most people don't argue with this response.

I wanted to answer right away, but my insecurities were front and center. However, I knew I couldn't refuse the offer. This was a job I so desperately needed, and I knew God was in it immediately. My inadequacy didn't matter.

The next few days were filled with an array of emotions. One moment I would be on the mountain of excitement remembering the words God spoke over me, and the next I was careening down the side, crashing into a valley of despair as I heard my own words. *Who do you think you are? You can't work for a church. You're not worthy of that position.*

I truly believed only those who were well groomed in the Word, had all the answers, and lived picture perfect lives could work for churches. Being the opposite of this, I never dreamed someone would ask me.

I had no prior credentials that qualified me. I certainly was not offered the job because I knew someone who knew a guy. Instead of remembering the "God said", I focused more on my inability, lack of qualifications, and dysfunctional personal life. I was in no state to take a position at a church! These thoughts tried to choke out my yes.

But wait a minute, God said I would do this! I had to remember above all else, that He set me up! I didn't have to understand or know everything. I just had to be obedient and say yes. He would take care of the rest! I'm so thankful God doesn't call only those qualified to do His work. Instead, He qualifies those He calls.

As I pondered this strange job offer, I asked the Lord, "Why me?" to which He simply replied, "My ways are not your ways" (Isaiah 55:8). Oh yea, I had forgotten that. Okay then, let's do this.

This brief conversation with my Father in Heaven helped me to take the next step of obedience, even though I didn't understand. I grabbed my Bible and looked up the verses around this truth for more confirmation. Isaiah 55:11 was the verse that sealed my questioning mind. "So will the words that come out of my mouth not come back empty-handed. They'll do the work I sent them to do, they'll complete the assignment I gave them" (MSG). I remembered the words He spoke to me driving down the road that day in California. "You will work for my church." And it was so.

It was only God who made it possible, and little did I know, He was giving me more than just a job. He was giving me an opportunity for growth and to cultivate relationships with others who would help to strengthen me and hold me accountable. He was positioning me to experience what real grace looked like. He was showing me how to be loved, even in my complicated mess.

This was far more valuable than any salary. The real benefits of the job were not a 401k, insurance, and income. It was learning to trust the sovereignty of God while experiencing unconditional love and acceptance. Instead of just leaving me outside the camp to figure it all out on my own, to only be invited in once I had, He brought me in. And He sent imperfect people to model before me the things He wanted me to learn.

I was one of His own; chosen, adopted into the family of Christ without the need to be an accomplished person in the eyes of the world. I only needed to be me.

14

UNCOVERING LIES

Lies are barriers to relationship. When someone we trust lies to us, we feel betrayed, angry, or even humiliated. If that person is a habitual liar, it will lead to a breakdown in relationship. Once trust has been severed, we have two choices to make. First, we must forgive. Forgiveness doesn't mean keeping the repeat offender around to continue hurting us. It simply means we release them and the offense to God. Second, we must decide if the relationship can be repaired or if it's better to move on without that person in our lives.

It's easy enough to remove ourselves from unhealthy relationships with others, but what if it is our own *self* causing the issues? I've heard it said that we are our own worst enemy. There is much truth in that statement. I'd been in a self-sabotaging relationship with myself for many years. So, if we are continually lying to ourself, how do we get away from that? What if we don't recognize that what we are believing is even a lie?

For example, maybe you've experienced a parent or teacher direct undue criticism or harsh words at you. Anytime you fall short of their standard, they tell you that you will never amount to anything in life. You've heard it so often that you believe what they say. This lie has become your truth. Anytime you experience failure, those words echo and are validated in your mind. *You'll never amount to anything! See? They were right. I'm no good and I can't do anything right. Look how messed I am.* And just like that, someone else's perceived opinion of you has now become your own.

Unintentionally believing a false identity and agreeing with it, is lying to yourself. However, we don't recognize that we are doing this because we believe it to be true. A lie only has the power to become reality when we believe it. What we believe, we become. If we believe the false identities placed on us by others, we are enabling them to be true. I have experienced this "self-fulfilling prophecy" effect many times in my life.

I've never been a thin person. I began eating my emotions around the age of eight and never stopped. Many who were close to me and some who were just school bus bullies called me fat. The ones closest to me were the ones that caused the deepest wounds. Even though I was overweight, how it was brought to my attention was not done in a way of concern for me, but in a way that said I should be ashamed of myself. I adopted the belief that being fat was ugly and shameful. I began looking in the mirror and staring at my stomach, hot tears of pain running down my cheeks. I'd grab handfuls of fat and squeeze as hard as I could while saying through gritted teeth, "I hate you. You're so fat." Standing there in the bathroom, I would imagine taking a knife from the kitchen and cutting my fat rolls right off. Instead, I'd head to the kitchen to find something to eat.

The truth was, I was overweight. The lie was that I was ugly and should be ashamed of myself. I was not encouraged to lose weight for my health, only for outward beauty. I resented that and continued to eat! My bathroom routine continued for years and eventually, every time I glimpsed my reflection, I said, "I'm fat," and immediately looked at whatever part of my body was the biggest. I was becoming who I believed I was. I couldn't lose weight no matter what I tried. Simply repeating the phrase "I'm fat" had the power to keep me in the very place I didn't want to be. Unhealthy and overweight!

Even if I needed to shed a few pounds, it was going to be much more difficult to do so when I continuously called out in myself what I wished to change. Telling myself how fat I was over and over led me to other thoughts of self-hatred and disgust that kept me going back to unhealthy food to drown out my sorrow about being fat. There's a line in an Austin Powers Movie that I chuckled over at first but then really thought about how true this was to me: "I eat because I'm unhappy and I'm unhappy because I eat."

Words are powerful and can shape our present and future. These words can be spoken words or just thoughts. Henry Ford said, "Whether you think you can, or you think you can't—you're right." I wanted to think like *The Little Engine that Could* and believe I could do anything. But instead I believed the lie that I'd been told, "You'll never be anything without me, you'll never do anything without me, and you'll never have anything without me."

Lies are a powerful weapon of deception. The enemy of our soul watches and waits for any opportunity to drive these seeds deep into our identity. He leaves no opportunity missed. Not one. The seed takes root once we believe it. Even if only a little.

Many of the lies I believed about myself were planted because of abuse, abandonment, or rejection. I filtered everything through the lens of pain and disappointment. These negative thought patterns were shaped based on the messages I received from those who were supposed to love and protect me. When something terrible happened, I would blame myself and hear the whispering lie that I believed to be true. These beliefs guided my decisions. They drove my inability to feel valued.

The feeling of worthlessness came first from the sexual abuse. The lie became deeply rooted when I was used and tossed aside by someone I believed to be my daddy. Other events happened that would confirm that message in my heart time and time again. Some were small circumstances that would lend to the lie, some were large devastations. Never experiencing the love of a father cut deep. How could I be of any value knowing that I had a biological father out there who didn't love me either? Why was I so unlovable? What was wrong with me? The answers to those questions came straight from the enemy of my soul. The lies' roots expanded even deeper and grew wider.

Picture an enormous oak tree. The trunk is thick and strong; the branches teeming with life; the canopy providing a reprieve of shade. The root system lies just eighteen inches under the soil of this large tree, expanding down first with the taproot then out horizontally to give it strength and nutrients.

Sometimes, instead of the roots growing down and then out as they should, they wrap around the base of the trunk and restrict the flow of water and nutrients. If caught soon enough, it can be easily corrected. However, there are times when it goes unnoticed until the tree exhibits signs of illness. The tree will die unless the foundation is healed. Untangling these wrapping roots can be difficult, but it can be done. It takes the skilled hand of one who knows the root system.

When a lie is planted in our heart, like a weed in a bed of flowers, it can go unnoticed if the garden isn't tended well. Once the lie takes root, it alters the landscape of our belief system and we unknowingly begin making choices based on the lie. Each time we agree with it, it grows deeper and stronger. We water it with agreement, fertilize it with resentment or ignore it altogether. The roots form without us even noticing. They interlace with one another, grabbing a hold of the roots of other lies, circling, and squeezing the joy and life out of us.

On the surface, what is growing is a distorted image of what was supposed to be. The lie suffocates the flow of nutrients and causes us to look like something we were never intended to. Only with the help of the skilled hand of Holy Spirit can we recognize these intruders, pluck them out and allow Him to work on our foundation.

I had to establish a new root system, but I can't fix what I can't see. The only way to do this was to invite Holy Spirit to show me where to start (Psalm 139:23-24). The enemy lied to me and I accepted those lies as truth for so long that now I had a sick root system. The effects were apparent on the surface of my life. I was made to be strong and fierce, brave and bold, yet my life reflected anything but the image I was made to be. From the beginning, the enemy threw assaults at me. The lies that I believed shaped who I thought I was. I had unknowingly assumed a false identity.

My foundation was built of lies. Low self-esteem, anxiety, depression, negativity, and anger were the mortar holding the bricks together as I built a fortress, caging myself inside. Every decision I made came out of one of the many rooms inside this fortress.

God offered to partner with me to burn the forest of lies and start replanting the soil. He was calling me out of this place of defeat and into the garden where he was planting seeds of truth and victory! He watered them with His Word, cultivated them with love and poured light over them from the Son who brings life from death.

TRUST

God knew I wouldn't trust Him to help me with this at first. He graciously sent beautiful mentors and friends who would help me tear down the fortress around my heart. Demolition days were the toughest! With God's help, we smashed the false sense of security I built to protect myself.

Walking the path of healing is not an easy road. The lies I believed wouldn't just be undone with the snap of my fingers. They wouldn't change because I looked in the mirror and recited personal affirmations. Rather, it took great effort to face the pain and uncover the deep trauma imbedded in my heart.

The idea of being healed was much more appealing than the reality of doing it. I was undergoing physical therapy for my soul. The pain after an injury is terrible, but the pain associated with physical therapy to heal the injury can be worse. Just like any physical therapy routine, if you don't do what you're told to in order to heal, you risk not healing properly. You may never regain your strength or the use of the area that was injured if you don't do the hard things.

My wounds festered for so long, they were infected, creating a stench that permeated my thoughts and reflected in my attitude. When the Lord showed me areas that needed healed, at first, I would beat myself up. I wondered, "How did you let yourself get here?"

In reply to that thought came the loving reminder that He was the healer and would help me. It was not up to me alone! Healing is a decision and takes effort! I knew no one was going to do it for me. I had to decide for myself if I wanted it. Then I had to choose to partner with God and allow Him to work. My job was to be willing to let him.

FEAR

Satan used fear as his main weapon of choice to keep me in my self-imposed prison. Like a dog that its former owner had beaten, I kept my head down and my tail tucked under when I first came to know God. Even though I wanted to trust Him, I didn't.

I believed the lie that God would hurt me if I got too close. I feared He would not love me just as I was. I flinched at the hand of love, for fear it would hurt, and honestly... sometimes it did. When I needed to be corrected for my attitude or actions, it didn't feel good. Not because God was harsh, but because I was painfully aware of my need for change.

God never beat me with condemnation, but gently convicted my heart to look at the things I needed to address. This is love. Love will tell you when you have bad breath or something is stuck in your teeth, right? Love will see you in the mud pit and refuse to join you. Love will pull you up and not let you stay there!

Fear was losing its place because perfect love casts out all fear (1 John 4:18).

DISCIPLINE

"Now all discipline seems to be more pain than pleasure at the time, yet later it will produce a transformation of character, bringing a harvest of righteousness and peace to those who yield to it." (Hebrews 12:11 TPT)

If you are training to strengthen your muscles and you haven't been to the gym in a while, you will feel the pain of disciplining your body. Healthy discipline can be uncomfortable, but in the end will produce a benefit.

Discipline and correction can save our life. Because I love my children, I wouldn't stand by silently while they drove off a cliff. I would jump in the vehicle's way with all the strength of Superman, stop it and turn it around. I would do everything in my power to course correct. This is what God wants to do for us if we will allow him.

You may read this right now and thinking to yourself, "Great, I already drove off the cliff. How can God fix this wreckage?" You are so loved that there is no disaster He cannot help you out of. Nothing is too messy or too far gone for the One who can do exceedingly and abundantly far more than all we ask or think because of the power that resides inside of us through the Holy Spirit and our Lord Jesus Christ (Ephesians 3:20). God is a good and loving parent.

"My child, don't underestimate the value of the discipline and the training of the Lord God, or get depressed when he has to correct you. For the Lord's training of your life is the evidence of his faithful love. And when he draws you to himself, it proves you are his delightful child." (Hebrews 12:5-6 TPT)

15

THE EXCHANGE

At first, I couldn't trust that God was a good Father. I could not refer to Him as Father God at all. I could only call Him God. Any term relating to a father made me feel distrust and abandonment. I saw modeled before me fathers that hurt, lied, left, cheated, blamed, and punished harshly. The word "Father" didn't invoke feelings of intimacy and acceptance. Once I learned that my step-dad was in fact not my dad and I had a biological father out there somewhere, I struggled to understand why he hadn't rescued me. Why didn't he come back and get me? Why didn't he want to be in my life at all?

I believed my dad left me because I wasn't good enough. The story I had been told about why my dad left was one that was no fault of my own, but I still felt the blame deep in my heart. How could he have left his child unless I was undesirable? Maybe he wanted a boy?

However, I couldn't shake the feeling that if he were alive, maybe he would want to know me if only we could meet? I searched with the only evidence I had been given, his name and one picture. I used Google and Facebook a few times, but to no avail. Each time I looked and found nothing, I figured it was just the way it needed to be. Honestly, I didn't search very hard. I knew I could have hired help, but secretly I was afraid that if I found him, he would reject me. No, maybe it was best I didn't find him after all. I shoved the nagging "what if" deep into the recesses of my heart and locked it away.

In the later years of my marriage, I often wondered if things would have been different if I had my father in my life. Would he silently ignore the injustice and abuse I was enduring, or would he swoop in and rescue me by giving me the courage to move on? Part of me wanted a father who was a knight in shining armor, and part of me was certain he wouldn't be. Maybe it was better left alone. I had lived without him this long; I would be fine. Or would I?

One evening, the children and I attended a wedding of a friend. It was everything you may imagine a wedding to be like. Beautiful and full of family and supportive friends. My seven-year-old daughter was enthralled with the magic of it all. She squealed with excitement as she waited to see the bride in her princess dress. As customary, the father of the bride walked his daughter down the aisle to give her to her soon to be husband. As he stood holding her hand, he released the most heartfelt and magnificent speech of love. It was short, and the tears were many.

My little girl clutched my arm and whispered, "Mom, did your dad do that when you married Dad?" I hushed her, explaining we'd talk later. Secretly, I hoped she'd forget.

On the car ride home, she asked me again. I explained to her I didn't know my real dad or where he was. "Why don't you look for him?" Christina innocently wondered.

Oh Lord, help me explain, I silently prayed, "Baby, I have looked. I checked the internet a couple of times, but I don't know where he lives or if he even wants me to find him."

"I think you should try harder because I know if he met you, he would want to know who you are."

"Okay, sweetie. I will look for him again, but I can't promise I will find him."

"Mom? I hope you do. Cause if you do, I will get to have a grandpa." These were precious words from my daughter who usually says what she is thinking.

As we sang songs on the drive home, I thought about what she shared and my promise to try harder. I thought about how much it meant to her to have a grandpa. She didn't have one. Who knows, maybe she was right? Maybe he would want to know me?

After tucking the children into bed, I started my search. Grabbing my iPhone, I went outside to stare up at the night sky and ask God to help me be brave. As I thought about where to even start, I felt impressed to begin with Facebook. Sure, I'd looked there before, but it was worth a shot.

I knew what he looked like because I had a photo of him at age seventeen. We were practically twins. Even as I looked for a more aged version, I was sure his eyes would be the same. I typed in his name. Several people showed in the search bar, but none of them were him. I typed in various versions of the name, but still no luck. After sifting through an endless sea of faces, discouragement set in. I decided to attempt one more thing and then call it a night. I hadn't tried using his full name and as the list populated, there staring back at me, was my father!

I was shocked! My heart beat wildly with excitement! *Now what?* I stared at his face, studying his eyes, cheeks, nose, and smile. It was definitely him. August 31st 2014, at the age of thirty-two, I found my dad.

I sent him a private message that started with my name and who my mother was, followed directly by, "I don't want anything except to know you and to be known by you…"

I slept horribly that night, waking several times to check messenger. I fought off thoughts that he would reject me. If he wanted to find you, he would have by now. Do you really think he wants you to mess with him now after all these years? He looked so happy with his wife. Maybe she didn't know about me, and he wanted it that way.

The next day I went to church just like any other Sunday, except my mind was far away. I compulsively checked messenger wondering if there would be a response. I didn't want to tell my children I found him until I knew he wanted to know me.

After lunch, I checked one more time and then determined I would put my phone away and go play outside with my children. I opened Facebook for what seemed like the hundredth time and there on the messages section glowed the green dot to say, "You've got mail." Nervously, I clicked the icon. There it was, his reply! I couldn't believe he wanted to talk to me! He gave me his phone number and let me know to call anytime.

Screaming and jumping around in circles in my kitchen like I had just won the lottery definitely grabbed the attention of my children and they came barreling in.

"Mom! What is it? Are you okay?"

"Yes! I found Grandpa, and he wants to know me! He told me I can call him right now!"

There was such a great healing in my heart that day. We talked for most of the afternoon, asking each other questions. I listened to what happened between him and my mother. As I listened, I realized for the first time that it really wasn't my fault. I accepted that truth this time. I hung up feeling loved, cherished, and wanted. It was like getting a shot in the arm of something I had never experienced, and I loved the way it made me feel.

After that day, we talked often. There was a lot of catching up to do. The conversations were not always easy ones as we learned of the pain that each lived with. After many discussions of forgiveness and the love of God, the hard edges of pain softened. The scab was ripped away, revealing wounds in both of us. Now, the true healing could begin. Forgiveness and love were the ointment needed to properly heal areas in us we weren't even willing to touch.

Not one conversation went by in those next few weeks that wasn't sprinkled with talk of seeing one another. The phone was okay, but we had to meet in person. As I waited nervously in the driveway for his car to pull in, I wondered what it would be like to finally see him in person. *How is it going to feel to hug this man? Will it be awkward? Pacing the porch, I prayed. Let this encounter be a blessing. Help me feel comfortable and be real. I ended it with please help Jerry behave, AMEN.*

One month after connecting via social media, we were looking at each other face to face for the first time since I was six months old. The joy of that day far exceeded any of my expectations. This was a dream come true!

I had waited for this my entire life. Even before I knew he existed, I dreamed of being held by my daddy in a safe way. This was the day I would feel the arms of a man wrap me in love and safety without a concern that he wanted something more. We stood in the driveway and held each other, only releasing our embrace to study each other's faces.

The overwhelming acceptance of my earthly father portrayed an image of my Father in Heaven who loved and cherished me even more. God used my dad creatively to heal parts of my heart I couldn't before then.

16

LOVE CHANGES EVERYTHING

Through my relationship with my dad, I discovered what it meant to be a daughter and belong. This realization shifted my relationship with God the Father as well. The things I struggled with before became easier to accept. My confidence that He loved me, would never leave me, accepted me, wanted to be near me, and that I was His daughter, grafted into the family of the Kingdom of God, grew.

Faith is believing what you can't see. I struggled for so long to believe that God could be trusted because I doubted who He said He was and what He said about me. I could believe it for someone else, but not entirely for myself. God saw my brokenness, and He wasn't angry, but He would not allow me to stay there.

God used my earthly father as an example of His perfect love for me. He showed me what the love and acceptance of a father looked like so that I could grasp the love, acceptance and provision that was available through Him… my Heavenly Father. My earthly father was imperfect and only capable of expressing love as best as he humanly could, but my Heavenly Father is perfect, and He loves perfectly.

He showed me by example that His word is true, "So if you sinful people know how to give good gifts to your children, how much more will your heavenly Father give good gifts to those who ask him" (Matthew 7:11 NLT). How could I doubt His goodness now? I had a closet full of lies I believed about God and myself that needed to be cleaned out! The purge began with the example of my earthly dad's acceptance. I needed God's help to get in the back of my old wardrobe of lies, remove them, and replace them with the truth of His Word.

I was in training to be a strong warrior who would be the catalyst for change in my bloodline, but how was I going to do that if I continued to fill my mind with doubt? I needed fuel that would give me strength and that would only come from spending time with my Heavenly Father. Anytime I would go back to my old junk food habits of self-defeat and victim thoughts, I had a choice. Either I stayed there with my Ben & Jerry's on the couch, or I could throw on my proverbial running shoes and sprint to His arms where He could once again speak truth.

Changing a habit is tough if you don't have a new one to replace it. Since we are creatures of habit, there must be a plan in place when the old habit rears its ugly head.

I started smoking cigarettes at eleven. It was just a thing I did, part of who I was. I labeled myself a smoker and couldn't imagine what life would be like without that little getaway in my hand. It was my reprieve and sanity, or so I thought. It was harmful for me, but I refused to acknowledge this for far too long. I believed the lie that it calmed me down and helped me cope with life, when in reality, it was causing more stress on my mind and body. It was hurting my lungs, my cartilage, my brain function, causing my skin to wrinkle and gray, it smelled awful, and the list goes on. We know what the Surgeon General says, right? I finally realized I had believed a lie and had to kick the old habit to the curb.

Once I decided that this habit must go, drastic measures had to be taken to keep it from returning. So, I made a plan. I took it to God and laid it at His feet first, then I called 1-800-QuitNow for coaching and used patches to help with the withdrawal. The thought of gaining weight because I quit smoking also caused me great concern, so I had a plan to cover this too. I knew the habit of hand to mouth was just as great as the actual addiction to nicotine was. I rolled up a Wal-Mart receipt and taped it together to be about the same size in diameter as a cigarette. I then stuffed toilet paper pieces in one end to keep the air from flowing too quickly when I would put it to my lips. Yes, I still chuckle at myself when I remember the extreme lengths I went to in order to be free!

To make matters more difficult, people who smoked and weren't supportive of my decision to quit surrounded me. I endured ridicule and snide remarks. Change also brought about seclusion when everyone else would go out for a smoke, and I stayed behind to avoid the temptation.

A lot of times when you decide to change, there will be someone or something trying to woo you back to the way things were. Changing the habit of smoking was much the same process I had to take to get free from the habit of "stinkin' thinkin'."

I had to have something in place when the desire to believe the lies returned. I combated the lies and old thought patterns with truth that either God himself shared with me personally or through His living Word.

This was a challenge because I had been so conditioned to think broken thoughts. My mission to become whole, healed, and healthy was not as easy as I hoped! Having my dad speak love and acceptance helped heal a vast chasm I had in my heart, but there was still work to be done.

This hopelessly negative, beaten down victim of circumstances was getting the deep cleaning she so desperately needed. This began by acknowledging that I had believed the lie and it was, in fact, just that, a lie. I then reflected on all the reasons I felt like I had failed and was not loved because of it. Writing them in my journal, I could see where I held myself in contempt when no one else had! God hadn't set me up to fail, but to succeed. My mistakes were not proof that I was a mistake! I was not the sum of all my failures! What good news.

SHIFTING TIDES

Life had given me every reason to throw in the towel. To stay angry and bitter would have been understandable. Instead of sitting on my excuses, I used them to fuel me to change. Making these necessary changes within myself didn't change the reality that I was still in a very unhealthy relationship. I was changing, but the situation did not. It got worse.

Even though meeting my dad was wonderful and healing, it also brought about a whole new set of problems within my home. Jerry seemed threatened by my relationship with my dad. During Dad's first visit, Jerry acted horribly and couldn't hide his true colors for more than a day.

As hard as I tried, I could not create the illusion of a normal life with this man. My dad and stepmom saw right through it. After being with us for only four days, Dad pulled me to the side and asked if it was normal that my husband didn't touch me or ever say

"I love you." Dad noticed that when Jerry came home from work, he'd grunt something resembling "Hey" as he walked through the house to change, then sit down on the couch to play video games for the evening. Dad noticed he ate in the living room while we ate together at the dinner table. He wondered if maybe it was just a weird week for Jerry. I wished I could have said yes. But no, this was my normal. Jerry didn't hug or show affection and certainly didn't shower me with terms of endearment.

His lack of manners frustrated me. He hadn't even tried to have one conversation with my dad. Of course, bringing this up ended in a huge explosion of cussing and something about how my dad wasn't welcome back in his house ever again. He gave no reason, only that he didn't like him.

The next day, my dad checked out of his hotel. What should have been a week filled with joy ended up packed with drama. It emotionally exhausted me as I tried to referee and keep the peace at home while convincing my dad I was alright. By the end of the visit, he voiced his concern for the children and me. Even though I tried painting the perfect picture of marital bliss, he didn't buy it.

In tears, I watched as my dad drove away. It wasn't supposed to be this way! I was spent. There was nothing I could do. I was finally convinced we would never be normal, and that Jerry would never change. I just had to stick it out until my children were eighteen so they wouldn't be without their dad. This was the last line of reasoning I kept in my arsenal to pull from when things got really hard to handle. I had to stay for the kids, but once they were grown, I was done!

Looking back at this reasoning, I laugh. What was I thinking? Trying to wait it out for their benefit was doing more harm than good. I was afraid of leaving and risking his absence in their life.

It took a while, but I started analyzing the other side of my reasoning. What if I left, and they were better off? Staying for their sake was only modeling a life of abuse. I was inadvertently teaching them abuse is okay and they should put up with it. I had to show them it wasn't. If I wanted the buck to stop with me and the cycle of abuse to end, I had to stand up and not only *say* "this is wrong" but also *do* something about it!

God was aware of what I was dealing with. He saw how many times I tried waiting it out to see if change might come. He knew fear ruled my decisions, and that I didn't believe I could ever stand on my own. I had many opportunities to say, "No More!" Yet, I kept going back to the familiar. I wanted to be treated with kindness and dignity, so I fell for the grand promises of change every time. But the tide was about to shift and when the tide shifts, there's nothing we can do about it. On the horizon was yet another choice for change. A choice that would finally loose the chains of fear that bound me.

"Embrace uncertainty. Some of the most beautiful chapters in our lives won't have a title until much later."—Bob Goff

17

GREATER CHANGE

I woke to the sound of my daughter squealing, "It snowed mom, come see it!" Snow days were very exciting to my seven-year-old. I leaped out of bed to join her, but as I did, a sharp, burning pain in my groin stopped me in my tracks. Hardly able to waddle to the bathroom, I realized I needed to seek medical attention right away.

As soon as the roads were clear enough, I drove to the local walk-in clinic to be examined. I could never have guessed the words I'd hear next. "I believe you may have an STD. But we'll run some tests to be sure."

The verdict arrived. As I sat on the white paper sheet, the doctor explained to me I was suffering not from one but two STDs. The world seemed to come to a grinding halt. I could feel my chest tighten and the lump rising in my throat as I fought off the onset of hysterical crying. I immediately began trying to uncover any other possible explanation than the one I hated to believe. I asked all the necessary questions; could it come from a toilet seat, a towel or some other non-sexual encounter? The answers were not what I hoped for.

As I drove home, I felt numb. I knew I had not been unfaithful, so there was only one other explanation. Even knowing this, the same old thoughts welled up inside of me as I started sweeping it under the rug of my heart. I heard the familiar whispers saying, "You won't leave, you never do."

Reasoning that this must be a misdiagnosis, I resolved to get a second opinion. I called Jerry to share the diagnosis. I'm not sure what I expected, but it certainly wasn't what I heard next. When he began with, "Well, who did you sleep with?" I was devastated.

Defending myself only made the accusations and name calling worse. To diffuse the situation, I assured him I was going to seek a second opinion. We hung up, and I didn't see or hear from him for over forty-eight hours. Being alone gave me time to think.

I had uncovered evidence of unfaithfulness before. I blamed myself, at least in part, that I was in this position now. I was afraid I couldn't make it on my own, so I put the blinders on and stayed. Staying gave him permission to continue, and each time was a little worse than the last. I believed the lies even when I knew the truth. The truth had been too hard to look at, but no more!

My pastor's wife, Amy poured countless hours into me during our time working together. She constantly pointed me to what God says about me. She infused me with strength by accepting me just as I was, even after she knew what I was living with. She encouraged me to stay before the throne of Abba. I soaked up everything I could learn about who Father God was for four years.

I learned that if I filled my head with garbage, that's what would come out. So, I purposed to fill my head with life and truth. I was now fully confident that I was a daughter of God, made for more than this. There could be no more excuses. The call to action was to be brave and make the hardest decision of my life.

The next week I went to my OBGYN to get a second opinion for my assurance. I had spent the weekend making up my mind about what to do if the diagnosis matched. I pondered my future as I sat on crunchy white paper waiting for the door to open and reveal the truth. As the doctor came in, I could see pity in her eyes and before she spoke a word, I knew. She began with the medical jargon which I could barely hear through the screaming thoughts in my mind. I fought with myself to stay composed and not throw up. Even though I knew the truth in my heart, the confirmation brought with it a blow that felt like a sledgehammer to my chest. I still carried hope the first results were wrong.

After delivering the test results, I could tell my doctor was concerned. I could feel the heat on my cheeks and ears as I choked back tears. My hands were shaking, and I couldn't look her in the face. After a moment of complete silence, she asked, "How long have you been married?"

"We've been together for fifteen years!" I blurted out in frustration.

"Wow, that's a really long time. You must have been young when you got married," she replied.

Oh great, here we go with the small talk. I wasn't amused and really did not know where this was going. I squeaked out a quiet, "Yea. I was."

She continued, "Listen. There is only one way these are transmitted, so it was from your husband or another man. Has your marriage been strictly monogamous?"

"I don't know, but I haven't slept with anyone else in over fifteen years," I bluntly replied as I pushed away the urge to curl up in a ball and sob.

"Honey, if you didn't sleep with anyone other than your husband, then it only came from him. Has he been unfaithful before?" she asked.

Sheepishly, I replied, "Well… yes and no. I haven't caught him in the act, but he's been on the internet emailing women for years."

"Can you tell me more about that?" she asked.

"It's just messages with nude pictures and sometimes he answers Craigslist ads, but he swears he's never physically met any of the women," I nonchalantly replied. I was shocked at how natural it was for me to immediately defend him. I could tell by Dr. Smith's furrowed brow she wasn't buying it.

She thought for a moment before replying, "Do you have kids?"

"Yes, I have two."

"How old are they?"

"Eight and twelve."

"Okay, here's the thing. This time it's something we can give you medicine for and it'll go away. Next time it could be worse and there may not be medicine. Do you want to be around for your kids?"

There was no other way to answer but, "Yes!"

"Okay," she replied, "then if I were you, I'd be filing for divorce."

Whoa, wait... what? Did she just say that? I could tell the situation irritated her, especially once I started brushing off the internet stuff and trying to feed her the same lies I was trying to eat myself.

This was the nail in the coffin of my dream of ever having a healthy marriage. I'd endured all the second chances I could handle. There was nothing left. I had to think about my health and my future. How would I be a good mother if I was dead? What if she was right and the next time it was incurable? Just the thought of it overwhelmed me. I wouldn't stick around to find out.

18

DIAGNOSIS

In the six short months I'd known my dad, our relationship grew deeper. We spent countless hours on the phone getting to know one another; sharing all the joy and pain in the years we were apart. He listened to my love for God and asked questions that sparked wonderful conversations that led to a greater revelation of God's heart for him as well.

My dad often remarked about the type of person he believed I was. He saw something in me I didn't, saying, "Katy Rose, I can't believe you are so amazing. I've never met someone who has been through what you have and turned out as incredible as you are."

I would laugh and say, "Only God, Dad! It's only because of Him I am who I am."

I honestly didn't think I was that incredible, but I recognized what he saw and agreed. God in me is pretty amazing!

I'd been becoming who I was in that moment my entire life through a series of choices. I realized that I could have been in a very different place. I could have become what I witnessed growing up. I could have chosen alcohol or drugs to cope with the pain. There were multiple paths my life might have taken if I ignored that voice inside reminding me, "You were made for more!"

I am so grateful to be the one who portrayed God in such a way to my dad, but our relationship was not one sided. There was something we both needed that the other had. Love and acceptance, yes, but more than that, we needed healing in areas that only the other could help with.

My earthly father showered me with words of affirmation that Father God spoke to my heart years prior, but I had struggled to believe. These were words of affection, identity, and purpose that were now being affirmed. He pointed out my strength and ability to stand on my own, however, I knew it would never work if it were only up to me. If I tried to stand on my own ability and strength, I would fail.

I often followed up his great faith in me with my great faith in God. "I can't do it on my own, but with God's help, I can. If it were up to me alone, I would be in the fetal position on the floor."

At first, my dad didn't understand why I always brought God into the conversation. He didn't get why I wouldn't just take the credit due to me and be okay with it. The real reason was I needed to hear myself affirming that God was who He said He was. Sure, I might be pretty great, but God is greater.

When sharing my stories with him, I could always point to where God was in them. There was something happening within me as I heard my own voice speak about the care God had taken of me since childhood. Now, more than ever, I was going to need to pull from that reservoir of remembrance!

The startling blare of the 6:00am alarm began. I reached over and slapped the snooze button as usual, but only to silence it quickly to stop that awful noise. This particular morning, I didn't need the extra ten minutes. I was awake with anticipation as I planned my escape. I spent the night after the second diagnosis was confirmed, seeking God's direction for my next steps. Making my way to the coffeepot, I realized the following week was spring break. The perfect time to get away and look at my situation from a different perspective.

As I drove my sleepy-eyed children to school, I wondered if my dad would be up for house guests for the week. I had never been to New Jersey. Maybe it was beautiful in March, or maybe it would be blistery cold and snow all week. It didn't matter. I needed to be somewhere safe where I could think, pray and plan.

I waved goodbye and pulled out of the car rider line. My heart raced at the thought of sharing the diagnosis with my dad. I had precious little time while my children were in school to plan and prepare. I thought of all the obstacles I'd have to overcome.

My job didn't pay enough to afford my rent and all the other living expenses. I assumed I would live on state-assisted programs such as food-stamps and HUD housing. For so long, what I avoided like the plague looked like my best option. Even though I was willing to do whatever it took by any means necessary, I heard the Lord say I would not have to go that route. He gently whispered to me, "Remember, you are mine. No longer an orphan. I will not abandon you and your children will never be without what they need,"

Immediately, I remembered the promise in Psalm 37:25, "I have never seen the godly abandoned or their children begging for bread" (NLT). There was a great storm surrounding me, but when I kept my eyes on Jesus, the center of the storm, it was calm, with blue sky overhead. Peace swept over me, and all was well. It was when I took my eyes off him and looked at the storm that I would panic and sink.

Each time anxiety welled up as I worried about how, what, when and where, I heard the whisper of my Father reminding me of His promises. "You are precious, far more valuable than rubies (Proverbs 3:15). The flowers don't worry about what to wear and the birds don't fret about what they will eat because they know I provide for them (Matthew 6:28). Daughter, you are far more important than birds and flowers. I will provide. Don't worry or be afraid (Isaiah 41:10). Don't be anxious about anything (Philippians 4:6). I have a plan and will take care of everything (Jeremiah 29:11). I only ask that you seek me in all your ways. Don't lean on your own understanding (Proverbs 3:5-6). Be still, sit quietly and listen (Psalm 46:10). I am singing songs of deliverance all around you (Psalm 32:7). I say you are chosen (1 Peter 2:9). Stand firm, be strong when destruction comes knocking on your door because you have built your foundation on solid rock. With Christ as its cornerstone, you will not fall (Matthew 7:24-27). You are more than a conqueror (Romans 8:27), equipped with every weapon needed to be victorious (Ephesians 6:10). I have rescued, redeemed and restored you. You are mine and I will never leave you."

Well, okay then! It's settled! Anxiety bows before the name of Jesus. "Hey Siri, call Dad."

After spending much of the morning unveiling the diagnosis and the truth about my marriage, Dad agreed that we stay with him to give me time to think about and plan for the next leg of the journey. By mid-afternoon, I had a confirmation email with airline tickets.

My Dad took care of every detail and financial obligation. He was the knight in shining armor I always dreamed he'd be! I felt a covering I had not known. A sense of security and safety formed within me as God whispered, "This is how I care for you."

My confidence was growing. Not my self-confidence, because I was certain I didn't have what it took to go through with what needed to be done, but my God-confidence. In the past, darkness covered any vision of living a life of freedom from abuse. I just couldn't see it. When I would try to envision this free life, one of peace and security, I couldn't see past fear and doubt. It's impossible to walk confidently where you can't see.

This time, instead of seeing darkness as I peered down the path of my future, there was light. Although I couldn't see the entire way, I could see hope for a future, and that's all that mattered. God only asked me to take one step at a time and trust him to light the next. Even if it appeared I was taking a step off the edge of a cliff, he reminded me he was faithful and would place a sure path under my feet with each step into the unknown. If I was going to see Him move in my life, I had to start walking. I knew if I kept doing the same thing I had been doing; I was going to get the same results, or worse.

The flight back to Kentucky was filled with nervous energy as I thought about what I was embarking on. My exodus! The time I spent at Dads didn't give me an exact road map to get out, but it gave me the confidence that I needed to make the decision that had to be made. I didn't have all the answers, but I had the revelation from God to just take one step forward and trust Him.

Before leaving to visit Dad, Jerry threatened to throw all my belongings out and change the locks. I wondered if I'd drive up and see my things laying in the ditch. If so, what would I do? Where would I go? These uncertainties swirled around me as I drove home. Upon arrival, it appeared the yard was clear. The locks hadn't been changed. I was thankful to find that he wasn't home when we arrived. As I opened the door, there stood a scene that shocked me.

A large, brightly colored banner hung across the entryway from the kitchen to the living room that said, "welcome home". I couldn't help but roll my eyes. What may have been a sweet gesture of genuine love in normal circumstances was nothing more than a manipulative ploy. One last attempt to change my mind and make it all go away. This banner was the proverbial flower apology.

I wished he was really the man who would throw "welcome home" parties because he genuinely missed his family or buy me flowers for no reason other than to say I was thinking of you today. What could have otherwise been a very sweet gesture left me annoyed. It would not work this time!

I had to get out, and fast. The longer I stayed, the harder it would be to leave. Even though I was clear about my intentions, I knew I had to make plans and implement them quickly or Jerry would think all would be swept under the rug, yet again. He never took me seriously and really, who could blame him? I put up with so much already. Where was the limit?

Over the years of tenaciously seeking who I was created to be and gaining a sense of self-worth and value as a daughter of God, I was still missing one thing. Boundaries. I hadn't learned how valuable they were or how to implement them in my life. It wasn't until the last piece of the puzzle was put into place that I discovered where mine were and why they were important.

A year before my diagnosis, I discovered the world of boundaries while attending marriage counseling. Our therapist only knew a small portion of the problems and nothing of the abuse, yet she could clearly see there were boundary problems.

We sat on opposite ends of the cold couch in silence, waiting for the counselor to arrive. My thoughts swirled. *Isn't this what you wanted? Didn't you beg for this for years? He's here, now what's your problem?* The problem was no change was taking place in the home.

Going to counseling was something he agreed to after I found evidence of infidelity again via the internet. I had been asking for years to go to marriage counseling and the response was always the same, "You go! You're the one who needs counseling."

However, after discovering his profile on a vulgar website he carelessly forgot to erase, he was certain I was done, and I was. That's when he threw out the idea of marriage counseling in a last-ditch effort to sway me to stay. How could I say no? I'd been asking for this for years and now he was willing. I felt obligated. Maybe this would fix everything!

Unfortunately, after several sessions, I could see this was nothing more than a meeting he showed up for to put a check in the box. There was no intention to actually transform our marriage. Honestly, it couldn't be changed without complete transparency, and I was afraid to share the deep pain he'd caused from verbal and emotional abuse. I was nervous to share about his infidelity.

Frustrated at the lack of change, I finally shared something real. As far back as I could remember, there was no telling Jerry "No". If he wanted to do it, it would be done. If he wanted me to do something, I better do it or pay. He manipulated every situation I wanted to say "no" to in order to get his desired outcome. My agreement may not have come out as "yes", it usually sounded like, "Whatever," "Sure, if you say so," "Okay! Just leave me alone so I can sleep!" Or it could have looked like me staying, allowing the mistreatment, or not standing my ground when things were wrong.

After listening to us that afternoon, our counselor recommended we go through a book together, *Boundaries: When to Say Yes, How to Say No to Take Control of Your Life*, by Dr. Henry Cloud and Dr. John Townsend.

This book changed my life in ways I never expected. I learned why I built walls and how to tear them down and replace them with fences. Fences that have gates to allow people in. Most importantly, I learned how to say no, even when it wasn't what the other person wanted to hear. I learned how to stick to my decision and not wavier just to make them happy or to avoid conflict. I began to understand the effects of saying yes when I should have said no to please everyone else. It was time for some serious self-evaluation, and this is never easy, but always worth it.

When I held up the mirror, I saw an angry woman who was bitter from years of saying yes, when I should have said no! I put everyone else's needs, desires and to-do lists above my own. The problem with not being able to say no was that each time I said yes, I got angrier. I felt it was other people's fault for not being considerate of me or my time. In reality, it was up to me to create and stick to healthy boundaries. No matter who liked it! I had a realization that even if someone gets upset; it wasn't the end of the world. They would be okay!

In the case of my unhealthy marriage, my no always meant yes. So no matter how many ways I said "no", it was always perceived as yes. He expected that I would eventually do whatever he wanted. I had no real boundaries in my life until this point, so of course he'd think that. Now, instead of being afraid of his reaction to my boundary, I stood at the line of that fence and said "No."

No, I will not put up with this kind of treatment any longer.

No, I will not allow this to be swept away and ignored.

No, I will not accept one more empty promise.

Yes, I will stand up for myself.

Yes, I will provide a safe environment for the children.

Yes, I will make it!

Someone once said, information is power, but I believe information alone is not power. I believe having the information and doing nothing with it is a waste. Applied information is power, so I began to apply the information I'd learned in that book to help me move forward.

THE PLAN

I began by making two phone calls. The first was to the National Abuse Hotline to seek counseling and find out if there were any resources available to women in my position. For so long, I grappled with calling what I was living with abuse, aside from the times he was physically abusive. I wasn't certain his other behavior was abusive. The woman on the other end of that phone listened to my woes and as I ended my summary, I paused and asked, "I don't know if this is all considered abuse. Am I even calling the right place?"

This phone call further opened my eyes to what was otherwise a little blurry. The lines of what was and wasn't abuse were skewed.

The counselor began explaining what emotional and verbal abuse looked like and after hearing just a little of some of the most recent events; she assured me I was calling the right place. Although no resources were available to me through that program because of my rural location, that phone call assisted me in unexpected ways. I was even more certain that I had to keep going to get free from this.

The second phone call was to a precious friend who had the inside scoop on resources for people in hard places. She rattled off a list of places to call to find affordable housing. One man's name was my current landlord!

After spending the next week touring trailer homes with holes in the wall that reeked of dog urine and cigarette smoke, I panicked! The last trailer park I visited that day was the worst I'd seen so far. Not only were the living conditions not good, but the rent was off the chart to live in a place with broken windows.

Discouraged, I went to the Lord and cried. It wasn't the pretty kind of cry, no this was the snot slinging, can't breathe, eyes swollen shut kind of cry. I cried and repeated the same question over and over, "What am I supposed to do? I don't know what to do!"

Once there were no more tears left and I spent my energy, I lay in the silent darkness of my bedroom and heard the still, small voice inside whisper, "I am with you. Remember what I have already said." Almost immediately, I felt impressed to call my landlord in the morning. There it was! Direction.

The next morning, I paced the kitchen as I thought about what I was about to do. My landlord was known in our community as a farmer, land developer, and builder. More so, we knew him for being a grumpy, hard-nose, greedy man who gave nothing to anyone for free. When natives spoke of him, they never painted him in a bright light. Although he had never treated me poorly, I was nervous to call.

I had no choice but to call and let him know the house would be vacant in a month, regardless. Soon after I began my search for housing, Jerry decided he was leaving the area. He was determined to go before I found housing. He packed up, leaving me with only the children's things and my personal belongings. I knew he meant it when he said, "You came into this relationship with nothing, you'll leave it with nothing too." And I did. Only, he left me with the most valuable possessions, our children. That was all I needed and nothing else mattered!

Knowing that we'd paid rent for the rest of the month, I had precious little time to find a new home. As the phone rang, my heart beat out of my chest. *How do I explain? Lord help me!* "Hello," I heard the gruff voice of my landlord's answer. *No turning back now. You got this!*

I briefly explained the situation. After discussing the details and dates of moving out, I asked him the two questions I dreaded the most. Many other tenants had informed me that Mr. Landlord didn't give deposits back, but it was worth a shot. I figured I had nothing to lose by asking. The worst he could say was no.

"Sir, I need to ask. How easy will it be to get the deposit back on this house? I will clean it perfectly and even patch the nail holes. I am going to need it to move into another place," pausing only briefly to continue to my second question, "and I wonder if you may have something smaller available for rent for just my children and I?" *God, I need favor right now.* I prayed silently as I waited for his reply.

"Well…" he began in his slow, thick southern accent, "I would actually like to sell that house you're in right now. I'll tell you what. If you will let me put up a sale sign in the front and allow it to be shown while you're still there, I will give you $550 if it sells before you leave. You just need to make sure it's in good shape to be shown. If it don't sell before you go, just make sure the place ain't a wreck and I'll get your deposit to you."

I almost couldn't believe what I was hearing. He continued, "As for another place, I had one come open just this week. It ain't cleaned yet, but you could see it if you want. Now it ain't no house like you're in right now. It's smaller square foot, but it's three bedrooms and two bathrooms with a one-car garage attached. You wanna see it today?"

Let me explain why this was so incredible. Any time I'd ever heard people talk about Mr. Landlord, the most often quoted was, "He doesn't help anybody." But he was offering me a huge opportunity that I desperately needed at that moment. Besides regular homes, he owned land all over with smaller row homes that were 2-bedroom, 1 bath, coming in at around 500 square feet with no garage. He just so happened to have built three larger, row homes with 3 bedrooms and 2 baths at about 900 square ft with a one-car garage. One of the three larger row homes in the entire county had just opened up and his places fill up right away. When you live in a rural area with very few apartment complexes and little to no rental options, things don't stay open long.

It turned out to be right around the corner from where I lived, so moving would be easier! As I pulled into the rock drive, my heart pounded wildly with excitement. *It's happening! I'm really getting free this time!* Without even seeing the inside, I was hopeful. As I toured the newly vacated home, the smell of cigarette smoke was prevalent, there were some pieces of flooring coming up in a couple of corners, the carpets needed cleaning and the walls left evidence of children who seemed to have ran out of coloring books and possibly napkins.

Mr. Landlord was quick to remind me that the place hadn't been cleaned yet, but assured me it would be. He'd fix the trim, but the rest was as is. I didn't mind. I could clean the carpets myself and I would cover the parts of the floor that peeled away once I found furniture.

The rent was affordable, and it was infinitely better than any other place I'd seen so far.

Before leaving, I asked if the walls would be painted to determine how soon I could begin moving in. I knew if they were painted, it may be longer. I already felt so blessed to have found this much favor. What more could I hope for? I certainly didn't expect what happened next!

Mr. Landlord thought a moment and said, "Well… if you want me to have them painted, the rent is $550, but if you want to paint them yourself, I'll rent it to you for $525." Sold! No paint required! I'll wash them. Isn't that what magic erasers are for, anyway?

I drove home elated! I didn't know how it would all work yet. I still had a lot to figure out, but as uncertain as it all was, I was unafraid. A new boldness rose inside of me. I was not backing down this time. I rested in knowing I would have somewhere to finally call my own.

I'd heard the words "I can't", one too many times. I could do hard things because I finally realized that it wasn't up to me to succeed. It was up to me to do my best and let God take care of everything else.

That evening, I knew I needed to have a very difficult conversation with the children. They knew their daddy had just left, but had no idea what was happening. Sharing with them was not something I took lightly. I knew I needed to choose my words carefully and be sensitive to their response. After all, this was the second time they'd be experiencing this type of thing.

Throughout the day, I prayed God would give me wisdom and the words to say to help them understand why mom and dad couldn't stay married anymore. I wanted to be careful to help them understand it wasn't their fault. After picking them up from school, we sat around the kitchen island having our regular snacks and chatting about our day.

Once I felt the timing was right, I began the daunting conversation. "Hey guys? I got to talk with you about something. It's pretty important." My daughter interjected, "Is it about you and daddy?"

"Well, yes honey, it is," I replied.

She continued with sorrow in her voice, "Is it about him being mean to you?"

My heart broke at that moment. I tried so hard to hide as much from them as possible and I failed. She witnessed him pushing me through a glass table in our living room when she was only five. It was the event she referred to as, "the time daddy chased mommy about the table."

One afternoon, I found myself pinned up against a wall while he held my wrists so tightly that later they bruised. He was screaming something in my face. The only thing I could think about was getting the kids to the other room. My nine-year-old son, David, took action, grabbing his sister and shuffling her to her room. I could hear her crying as I shouted for him to let me go. I wanted to console her and make it all stop!

The next thing I knew, David came running from the back bedroom and leaped onto the back of his dad to free me. It worked, but only at the expense of my son. He was thrown backwards onto the floor. Jerry swung himself around to face David with fists balled up and a look to kill on his face. I felt my worst fear was about to come true. He stood there looking at our son, who was lying on the hallway floor, afraid to move for fear that he would be knocked back down if he tried to stand. I immediately took action and put myself in the middle of them, distracting his rage away from our son and back onto me.

Fighting back the welling desire to punch him right in the face for hurting our child, I screamed, "Leave us alone! Get out! I am so sick of this." I had no idea how to diffuse the situation any longer. I was panicking and terrified.

"I'm not going anywhere," he shouted, "You go!"

As he kept shoving me nearer the front door, I was determined to not leave the house without my kids and kept fighting my way around him. I couldn't let him lock me out without the children.

"Oh, no you don't." he said, "You're leaving right now!"

He continued pushing as I fought back. Finally, he shoved me so hard I fell over the arm of the loveseat backwards into the glass coffee table, shattering it with my body.

And with that, it was over.

The look on his face was complete shock. It's a miracle, but there wasn't one scrape on my body. He backed down, went outside to smoke and left me to clean up the mess; the table and the children.

I cleaned up a little after calming the children. I wanted desperately to leave. I wanted to leave for good, but the imbedded broken record of thoughts played, "You can't. You won't. You haven't yet, so why now? Just deal with it. You want your kids to have what they need, right? Then shut up and keep your head down."

It was like fighting with myself because I knew this was unacceptable, yet I had no boundaries. I had accepted it for so long. When enough was enough?

Once Jerry was fully immersed in the video game I had previously interrupted, I quietly got the children into the car and went to the park. I wanted to distract them from what had just happened, but first I had to talk to them about it! I never wanted them to sit in silent pain. I tried my best to explain why Daddy does the things he does. Hurting people hurt people, right? He just doesn't know any better. Maybe he was hurt as a child and is angry because of that… and all the other excuses I could muster.

I've always talked to my children about everything, and I believe communication is so important, but talking was not enough. I thought I was doing more for my kids than my mother did when abuse occurred. She never talked to us about what was happening or asked how we were feeling about it. I wanted to be 100% in tune with my kids' hearts. I believed I could help them deal with the confusion and pain by acknowledging the behavior was wrong, apologizing that they had to see or hear it, and then praying for them. I was partially right. Prayer was incredibly helpful in shaping who they are today, but talking was not enough. I had to do something about it. I needed to take a stand and say, "No More!"

I thought I was doing what was best by sucking it up and putting up with the abuse. I believed I was teaching them the valuable lesson of forgiveness and sticking with your marriage. However, I was inadvertently sending a message that this type of lifestyle is normal and that abuse is acceptable.

Abuse of any kind is absolutely unacceptable in every case. Learning what abuse actually looks like and setting healthy boundaries is step number one to getting free from it. Whether it's from a spouse, parent, boss or a friend, it's wrong. I had to learn this and now it was time to help my children understand it so we could move on. I assumed no conversation was a "one and done" deal when we were discussing matters of the heart and the emotions attached to what was happening. I needed to guard them in the process from the fiery darts of the enemy would throw at them in an attempt to destroy their joy and steal their true identity.

I believe it's so important to be proactive with our children and offensive about the attacks they are facing. Praying with our children about the pains they experience is vital and the only way to do that is to check in with them often. Talking is becoming a lost art in families and I believe the distractions of life and our selfie-driven culture are the weapons of warfare in this area. While we are creating Instagram reels and scrolling through endless newsfeeds, our children are silently crying out for us to notice them.

To heal, we must feel, then deal. Giving them permission to feel pain, anger, regret, sorrow, and even excitement when they were ready was key to helping them deal with what was happening. It was all part of the healing process.

After a lengthy and emotional conversation explaining all the changes to come and why, it was time to plan the move with expectations of a better life. I assured them we would get through this together and, as always, I encouraged them to come to me with their thoughts and feelings so we could talk about them as time went on. I couldn't sugarcoat it anymore.

Divorce is hard for everyone involved, especially the children. I needed to be more in tune to their heart's cry like never before. And all this while trying to tend to my own wounds! I knew there was no way I could do it alone. I needed God's help, and I needed people!

19

PROVISION

I want to share with you just a few stories about how God took care of my physical needs during this transition. I feel this is the most important part of my story because it is highlighting Jehovah-Jireh, the God who provides (Genesis 22:14). These stories all spoke volumes about the love God has for me, and it was in these stories that I saw a side of God I had not known before. In this process of having to depend completely on God, I learned more about His character than ever before. I began to know God in a whole new way.

It's my hope that as you read these testimonies of God's provision, you see yourself in my place receiving all God has for you as well. Your story is different than mine and I am certain your circumstances are unique to you, but whatever it is you need, go to Him and ask. If it's what's best for you, He will give it to you and usually so much more than you ever expected!

The day started like any other: coffee, car rider lines and work. I sat at my desk, trying to focus on my tasks and push through as though nothing was happening. This is what I did all the time. I stuffed things, overlooked them, swept them under the rug, ignored them. Or at least I tried.

I knew I only had a few weeks to pack what we had left, clean our current home, clean the new apartment before moving in, and then there was still the actual act of moving. I had so much to think about and I needed help. As I stared at the computer screen with my calendar out and my to-do list attached, I felt it taunting me. How could I work? What was I supposed to get done with all of this on my mind?

Alone in my office, I laid my head on the desk and cried. *There is so much to do and think about God. I don't know where to start. I need help.* My biggest concern was money. I kept asking God to help me figure out the finances and confirm I was doing the right thing.

Sometime around mid-morning, my cell phone rang. It was an unrecognizable number and it could have been work related, so I answered, "Hello, this is Kathryn," I said in the most professional voice I could muster.

"Yeah, uh, hello. This is Mr. Landlord. I was thinking about your deposit for that apartment."

I instinctively braced for the worst. My stomach ached with worry. He continued, "I am going to just go ahead and take the deposit from your current house and move it over to the apartment and write you a check for anything over that amount, pending the house is in good shape of course when you leave. Is that good with you?"

Hmm, let me think. YES! This was wonderful news, as it meant I wouldn't have to come up with an additional deposit amount! I was shocked by this amazing favor.

We continued the conversation about logistics for the move over the coming weeks. As we wrapped up the final details and the call came to a close, something even more unexpected and incredible happened.

"One last thing," he said with a little unease in his voice, "I think that apartment needs to be painted. It looks pretty bad."

Uh oh! We had already agreed it would be left unpainted so I could pay less in rent. He was right though; those walls were pretty awful. "Okay sir," I replied, "How long do you think that will take?"

"Well, I wasn't thinking about having a crew come paint it. I was thinking you could paint it if you wanted," he replied. "You can paint it whatever color you want. Just go on down to the supply store and get what you want. Tell them to bill it on my account for the address. Just make sure you tell them you want flat paint."

Wait! What just happened? This was a hard-nosed elderly man that no one liked, at least as far as I could tell, who supposedly gave no one anything. He had just made life so much easier by adjusting how the deposit would work and not only gave me permission to paint my new little place, whatever colors I wanted, but he was going to pay for it! Oh, and without raising the rent at all.

I was astounded! God was opening the floodgates of favor and provision in ways I never saw coming. I received the confirmation I had just prayed for hours before.

That afternoon, I picked up seven gallons of paint. The walls were light gray, but I wanted color. After all we'd been through, I thought it was appropriate. I picked out blue for my son's room, green for my daughter's, yellow for the living room/kitchen, and a beautiful dark gold for the walls in my bedroom, bath and hallway. I wanted to make that little row home as comfortable and beautiful for my children as possible.

Over the next week, I painted every spare moment I had. I borrowed a ladder and supplies from a friend and got busy. I'm no Bob Ross and the closest I've ever been to being artistic was "color by number", but there is something so therapeutic about painting a wall. A sense of accomplishment sweeps over me when I see a room transform as the old is covered by the new. However, the real reason I needed this project at that moment in time was for the mindlessness of it. I could just grab a roller and paint with little thought. After taping up the baseboards and electrical outlets, the hard part is done. All that's left is to paint and ponder.

I painted alone. Not because no one would help, but because I needed the silence and time with God. I needed the space to crank up some worship music and allow the Holy Spirit to minister to me through song lyrics. I needed to contemplate God's goodness and provision. I had to hear His voice over my own.

It was vital that I replace my thoughts with His truth right away because my thoughts were full of defeat, fear, and uncertainty. The best way I found to do this was by tuning into others who encouraged and taught the Word of God wonderfully via podcasts. I couldn't rely on a message on Sunday to get me through. I often listened to podcasts for two or three hours a day; in my car, on a walk, in my office, going to bed at night. There had to be other voices dominating my thoughts to reprogram my "stinkin' thinkin'". My thinking had gotten me to where I was, so I knew it wasn't serving me well. My love of learning motivated me to change and find out what others knew that I didn't!

One of my favorite teachers of the Word is Joyce Meyer, she's been a role model for me since I was thirteen. Her "no nonsense, tell it how it is," way of teaching drew me. I've always admired her boldness and raw honesty about her past struggles and victories. I listened to her podcast for over two years and her messages challenged me and stepped all over my toes. They changed my point of view on so many things and gave me confidence to stand in the face of adversity. As I painted, if I wasn't listening to worship music, I was listening to Joyce Meyer.

Well, let me be honest here. Sometimes the podcast played, and I didn't really listen. It was my background noise as my mind drifted off to one concern or another at times. One evening, I was finishing up the last parts of my bedroom wall while Joyce spoke on the topic of trusting God. This was one of those times when it was really hard to focus on what she was saying. At the end of the week, I was exhausted both physically and emotionally, and I just wanted to be done. I wasn't giving too much of my mental energy to the positive teaching I needed to be listening to.

I stood on my ladder, reaching overhead to paint the recessed ceiling around the fan, half-way listening. Suddenly, I tuned in fully and in that moment; she shared a story that changed my life.

I listened intently as she shared a simple yet profound concept. Ask God for what you need. Anything! Nothing is too big or too small. She said, "Pray about it and make your requests known." She then shared a simple story about a time she asked God for something as small as a can opener. I don't remember all the details, but the summary of what she said is this: money was tight, and she needed a can opener, so she asked God knowing what the Word said about making your requests known (Philippians 4:6). The next day, someone blessed her with a brand-new can opener! Not just any can opener, but an electric one at that! The light bulb went off for me at that moment. With each stroke of the paintbrush, I turned my thoughts to God.

God? If you can give Joyce a can opener because she asked you, can you please give me furniture for my new home? Immediately, I felt impressed to be more specific, so I stopped painting, climbed down the ladder, and paced the floor while I thought. I began to list off the items I really needed and some I would just like to have.

Lord, please help me find a dresser, bed, couch, and a small table. Then God spoke to my heart, "Be more specific."

It wasn't enough to just ask for those things in a general way. I was being asked to divulge all the details, to tell Him exactly what I pictured. I had to be very strategic in placing furniture in my tiny space and knew that only certain sizes of furniture would fit. For instance, the kitchen was attached to the living room as though they were one room, so for there to be a table to eat meals at with my children, it would have to be small. I'd thought a really cool bistro table would be great. One that had drop sides that would change from circular to rectangular to save space if needed. So that's what I asked for. I added that I would like to have a black one if possible.

The other piece of furniture I cared about was my bedroom dresser. It had to be narrow, so I asked for a tall chest of drawers. I envisioned a Victorian style, solid wood, light brown, with five drawers. I'd been looking on Facebook Marketplace and found several that would be perfect, but they were all out of my budget.

The bed and couch didn't matter. I hadn't given those pieces much thought. However, there was one little thing I was really hoping God wouldn't mind me asking for. It seemed so silly and unnecessary, but I asked Him anyway. "God? I'd love to have hanging flowers for my porch. Purple is my favorite color."

There was just enough room to put up a basket or two. This was something I was sad to leave behind when I moved out of my current home. I loved coming home and seeing my hanging flower baskets dangling from the hooks above the porch. I enjoyed sitting outside and staring at them. It was something that brought me peace.

After making my requests known to God, I went home that evening and journaled each thing I asked him for. This was intentional because I wanted to continue to pray for these items and visualize what they would look like and where I would put them in my new home.

During this transition, my friend Ruby and her husband Dan came to visit me as they traveled through my part of the country.

This was the same friend who called me that memorable day to ask if I would like to be discipled seven years prior. It was a wonderful visit filled with laughter and encouragement. Confidence is built around people who love you for you, junk and all. Ruby and Dan are some of the greatest balcony people I know, always seeking to bless those around them.

I was sad to see them go but glad to have had to chance to take a moment and forget the craziness of my circumstances. As they drove away, I immediately went back to packing boxes. The paint was dry, the apartment was clean, and now it was time for the move.

After cramming every inch of my Chevy Malibu with clothes and miscellaneous items, I drove the few miles to my new place, hopeful and ready to get this part behind me! As I came up over the hill to see a full view of my apartment, I immediately noticed two flowerpots filled with purple and white pansies trailing down the sides hanging from my new front porch!

As I pulled into the driveway, my heart beat wildly with wonder! *Who did this? Where did they come from?* No one knew I wanted these but God! I stood outside of my car staring up at the swaying planters hooked beautifully in place and cried. I knew God was taking care of what I needed with the paint and making the deposit work out, but this was a "just because" gift! When I asked him for those three specific items, two I needed, and one I didn't, He gave me the one I wanted first! He showed me how important my desires are to Him as well.

God is a God of abundant blessing! He loves to give extravagant gifts to His children. Once I trusted Him and believed He could do it, I saw He would! There is a big difference between believing He can do it and believing He can do it for you. I used to believe He could do anything, but I didn't necessarily believe He would do it for me. I didn't feel worthy of His blessing or favor.

Those flowers were a kiss from my Father. I imagined the card He would have left with them. *I see you. Enjoy these beautiful flowers as a housewarming gift. LOVE, ABBA.*

Later, I found out my precious friends, Dan and Ruby, stopped by the apartment before heading out of town and left those for me. They had no idea I had just prayed for those, but God impressed on their hearts to do that. How wonderful it is to be used by God to bless those around us. We never know how our obedience will affect others. Dan and Ruby were an answer to prayer that day!

Moving in was a smooth process, thanks to the help of friends. We were adjusting to the apartment and the peace that came with it. Two weeks after we moved, I still didn't have a couch or dresser. I had a suitcase and blow-up mattress on the floor, but I was the most content I had ever been in my entire life.

Toward the end of the first two weeks, I received a phone call from Mr. Landlord. I wasn't expecting a call and was a little perplexed, hoping everything was okay with the former home. Turns out the agreement to let him list and show my home while I was in the process of moving out had paid off! He called to let me know the house was shown to only one man within that three-week period and he bought the home! He would send me not only the $550 check for the agreement but also the entire deposit would transfer over since I left the house in such great shape. This meant there was an additional $325 over the amount of the deposit needed for the new apartment. He would send me a check for $875. I was astounded yet again to see how the favor of God was at work in my life.

A week later, I received a message from a friend who had a couch she wasn't using anymore. Okay, couch, check that one off the list!

Another friend sent me a text a few days later asking if I could use a recliner. It would have to be small. I asked her for the measurements and checked them against the only space it might would work in. It was a perfect fit!

She offered to bring it to me the next weekend and had a couple of other items she wondered if I could use. A full-size bed and a bistro table. Before I could finish reading the text, she sent me pictures of the table. It was tall, black, round and had drop sides. It was EXACTLY the table I had imagined in my mind when I asked

God specifically for it. I was overwhelmed with gratitude! What made it even more awesome was that she didn't know what I asked God for.

Before the week was up, this same friend sent me a screenshot of a man who was giving away a Victorian style dresser, solid wood, light brown, with five drawers on Facebook Marketplace. It was FREE and exactly like the one I pictured in my mind when I prayed and asked God. God provided every single thing I asked for that night within one month. I could share countless other things God did to take care of me in this season, but I want to share just two more stories of God's provision.

It was a hot July morning as my children and I raced out of the house to get to my office on time. As soon as the driver's side door closed, I remembered something very important was still inside. I pulled the keys out of my ignition and handed them to my twelve-year-old as I asked him to run back in and grab the item I needed. After quickly explaining where it was, I hurried him along, reminding him to lock the door when he came out.

After a few moments inside, he emerged with the forgotten item and proudly waved it in the air as he locked and shut the door behind him. He ran to the car as quickly as he could, jumped back in the passenger seat and said, "Got it!" as proud of himself as can be. He loves to help his mom! I waited as he buckled up to leave. I held my hand out for the keys to the car, to which he replied, "What?"

"I need the keys, buddy. I have to start the car." Then I saw it, the look of sheer regret!

"Oh, mom! I left the keys on the table. I set them down and forgot to grab them again on my way out!"

I immediately called my employers to inform them of the situation, and then I called a local locksmith. I did not have the money to call a locksmith to break into my house, but it was that or break the window. I am sure the latter would have cost me more!

An hour later, we were back in the house. I paid the locksmith their fee which was half of my utility bill due in two days. Now that I paid them, I wouldn't be able to cover my electric bill in full. Up to this point, I'd done well to save and make sure the money was there for the necessities. I asked the kids to go inside so mommy could have a minute to herself. As soon as the door was shut, I melted onto the concrete under my hanging flowers and sobbed.

God, what do I do now? I don't have the money to pay for our utilities! After a few minutes, I pulled myself together, breathed in the warm morning air, and noticed the unusual number of birds around my driveway. As I stared at those birds pecking the ground, all of them fat and beautiful, I heard that still, small voice inside, "If I take care of the birds and they lack nothing, won't I take care of you and your children? Look at them. They are not fretting about where their next meal will come from. They just know it will come. Be still my daughter and know that I am God."

With renewed peace, I stood, brushed off my pants and went to work. The next afternoon, upon checking the mail, I noticed a small envelope addressed to me with no return address. I was so curious to find out what was inside; I stood at the mailbox and opened it. It was a small red, folded card with these words, "Just a note to say your utility bill has been paid. Have a great day. Your friend." Inside was a receipt with the paid balance for my records.

You might have thought I won a million dollars watching me jump around at my mailbox without a care about who was watching! Tears of joy, laughter, and excitement welled up out of me. I had not told anyone. Only God knew I needed the bill to be paid. And there it was, taken care of... just like the birds.

In the same month, I was serving at a Sunday morning service with our children's ministry. Our church met at a temporary location while we looked for a permanent home. It was the middle of July and unfortunately the A/C had gone out this day. The fans we had were not cutting it and as soon as service ended, we were all eager to tear down and leave. As I went from one task to another, trying to put things in place to pack up, a woman stopped me in the hall. She explained briefly that she didn't want to keep me from my tasks, but that God had asked her to give me something. She handed me an envelope. I thanked her, and we exchanged pleasant goodbyes. Being desperate to get out of that building, I didn't want to take the time to open it up right away, so I tucked it into my pocket and continued working.

As soon as I got to my car and cranked up the A/C, I reached in my pocket to retrieve what God had given me. I opened the envelope to find a check for $550. My exact rent amount plus $25 extra. Again, I could not contain my joy! I laughed, shouted, did a little happy dance in my driver's seat and shared the news with my kids.

All along the way, through every act of favor, I shared it with my children. I wanted them to experience God's real provision for themselves. After all, it was for them too!

I share these stories to shine a light on the lengths God will go to care for His children. I did nothing to warrant all this favor except seek Him earnestly with my whole heart, trust Him to take care of our needs, spend time in His presence, and commit to be as obedient as possible.

This obedience thing was an issue for me at first and honestly still can be! I rarely did what He asked me the first time, and I typically responded with, "no," or "I can't", before saying yes. My disobedience wasn't out of rebellion, but out of a heart of fear. My doubt and lack of trust caused me to be guarded. Once I purposed to let God in and give Him a chance, He showed up.

Of course, this doesn't mean I get everything I want anytime I ask. God isn't a genie in a bottle. But it does mean the Word is true when it says, "Delight yourself in the Lord and, He will give you the desires of your heart" (Psalm 37:4 ESV) and "When you ask, you must believe and not doubt, because the one who doubts is like a wave of the sea, blown and tossed by the wind" (James 1:6 NIV).

I had to choose a side. Either I believed His promises were true, and He is who He says He is, or I didn't. If we think God is good, we look for Him to be good to us. We believe, if He did it for them, He will do it for us, or we can choose the other side of the coin. I chose the latter for most of my life. Believing He could, but He probably wouldn't. Therein lies the barrier to receiving. My distrust and doubt caused me to forfeit many of God's promises. I simply wasn't open to receiving all He had for me.

Once I decided to throw all reservations to the wind, a great change occurred. Not only in my physical life with provision, but in my soul. I fully surrendered to God and said, "Have your way Lord."

I couldn't control anything, so I had to believe He was in complete control, come what may. He could do a significantly better job than I could. Trusting God doesn't mean we sit back and do nothing. Rather, we partner with God, doing all we can and letting God do the rest. Where I am weak, He is strong. He can do exceedingly, abundantly more than all we would hope or ask for (Ephesians 3:20).

Learning to listen to His voice for my next move was the most important thing I did to experience a desirable outcome… what I call favor! I prayed for wisdom, resources, and strength. Then I rested. This rest taught me to have peace. Peace unlike any this world can bring.

Things weren't easy. I still dealt with tremendous emotional pain, as it took months for my abuser to relent even after I left. But, even during great turmoil and uncertainty, I had peace. That peace came from staying under God's covering and burying my face in his chest often. Just like a child runs to her father for comfort when they've experienced pain and sorrow, I too ran to the Father. He was my safety in the storm.

The peace I carried didn't look like a tropical shore with sunny skies overhead and perfect 80-degree wind gently blowing on my face. No, this was the peace that is found in the eye of a hurricane. The storm is all around, on every side, yet the center is calm. This is the kind of peace I learned to walk in. The storm could no longer threaten me because HE was my protection and would make a way out.

20

SEEKING HELP

As my phone buzzed for what seemed like the hundredth time that day, I wanted to scream! I knew it was him. It had been a month now and Jerry didn't just disappear with the miles between us. Instead of in-person verbal and emotional abuse, it now came via text. The messages were documented proof of the types of things he said to me for years. One message would drip with regret and the next would damn me to hell. I finally got fed up with the Dr. Jekyll and Mr. Hyde act, and my responses resembled, "Stop texting me. I don't want to hear it." These were not the responses he hoped for, so he would ramp up the insults and threats.

After a while, I just couldn't take it anymore. The negative effects of his words were plaguing me. I wanted to be free of him and yet, here I was somehow still stuck in his web. It was time to find help!

I left my phone inside and sat on my front porch, reflecting on all that had been said that day and the days before. God was providing for all my immediate needs, but I was wounded within and needed more than material items. Even in my avid journaling, I found I was getting nowhere fast. There was too much coming at me and not enough energy to deal with it all.

As I stared out at the trees, my thoughts wondered. *God, I need freedom from this! I want peace. I am so tired of it!* Then my mind would drift in and out of whining about my situation. I wasn't directly asking God to take care of anything or guide me. I was just complaining.

This went on for quite some time before I realized I hadn't heard anything from God. Probably because I wouldn't be quiet long enough to hear Him anyway, so He silently listened. Oh, Lord! I'm so sorry. It's just so frustrating.

In the silence, I pondered how to find help for my mental health. Jerry threw so many lies at me to see which ones would stick. It was difficult not to doubt myself at every turn. *What if what he says is true? Am I just overreacting? What if I am all those names he's calling me?* I needed someone else to hear what was happening and tell me I wasn't crazy! Or maybe that I was. It didn't matter. I just needed help.

Eventually, my mind quieted. In the silence, I heard God speak. "If I asked you to adopt when you were forty-four, would you do it?"

Perplexed and a little frightened at the idea, I responded, "No!" and then silence. "Well, I don't know, maybe." More silence, "Okay God yes. I would! But why are you asking me this right now?" As if He didn't know my current situation.

He said nothing more as I heard my own words echo in my mind, "NO!" It was in that moment when I realized my auto response to being obedient, to any prompting He gave was NO.

Later that evening, I journaled about it and dug deeper into my heart to ask some hard questions. I wanted to be obedient and to trust Him, even if it was scary. Sure, I just did some really tough things, removing myself from the abuse and experienced God's amazing favor, but my auto response hadn't quite shifted yet. Did I desire to adopt? No. But it wasn't about that. It was about learning to trust God in everything.

I believe God used this seemingly far-fetched question to open my eyes to the apprehension in my heart. He was teaching me obedience to even the most extreme request or direction that may come from Him. He simply wanted my default to shift from no to yes and for it to happen more quickly. I later realized the importance of this and the freedom that comes from letting go and letting God. A phrase often quoted but less often walked out.

At lunch time the next day, my phone started buzzing with more manic messages. "Did you get the flowers? Silence. "Hey! Just let me know you got them." More silence. "Alright, I see how it is." Continued silence, "Go ahead and just throw them away. You don't care, anyway." What I wanted to throw was my phone!

My phone went off multiple times before the day was done, filled with messages calling me everything but for dinner. It was infuriating and mentally exhausting.

God, what do I do?! I need this to stop! I grabbed my pen and journal. *How can I deal with this anger welling up inside of me? I'm so tired of hearing the same old words. I hear what I know are lies, but I mildly accept them as truth. I don't want to go back. I want to forgive and move on, but how? I can't trust any of his words. God, guard me from deception and manipulation. I don't want to be a victim anymore. I need confidence and peace.*

God, you live in me. You gave me hope. You promised me a future. Not a future without adversity, but you promised you would walk with me through each trial and that you would never leave me. How can I be confident I am making the right choice? Help me walk in wisdom.

I don't want to be angry anymore! I'm tired of feeling like a worn-out rag doll. I'm done being afraid, alone, beaten, kicked, and taken advantage of.

Jesus, you bore all of this for me at calvary. Help me release and abandon my chains! Help me walk by faith, not by sight. You are the comforter of my soul, my help in need, my mighty deliverer. You are my rock, my source of life, my provider. Jehovah Nissi! You are my flashlight on a dark path; you light my way. When I feel confused, I will look to the left and to the right and hear your voice for direction. Help me be obedient.

I woke up to twelve missed texts! I couldn't ditch my phone because of work, but I had to figure something out. I needed this obsessive mental beating to stop. Taking steps to seek help in this new season was key. I was determined I wouldn't be trapped in a web of lies and deceit again because I was exhausted.

After coffee, I dialed the abuse hotline for the second time. The first time I spoke with a counselor, they were an enormous help in validating my situation. At the moment, they made me feel as if I weren't crazy. I didn't know if they could help with this situation, but I thought I would share what was going on to get counseling for ways to cope. Maybe they would have a suggestion about how I could get these obsessive messages to stop.

After speaking to a counselor for a few minutes, she strongly advised I seek a restraining order and assured me what I was dealing with was harassment. She validated my thoughts and gave me encouragement along with facts. It's hard to see situations clearly when the lines have been blurry for so long. I needed to hear logic over emotion. I was not in a place to be making reasonable decisions. Mental exhaustion was taking a huge toll on me.

The next step was to seek legal assistance. A lawyer was going to be out of the question, although I knew I needed one. I didn't have the money to afford attorney fees or court costs. My finances were tight with very little wiggle room.

Explaining my financial situation to the counselor, she suggested I reach out to legal aide to assist. After gathering all the necessary information, I hung up that day with a renewed sense of relief and direction. The very next day, I had an appointment.

The smell of aged, musty carpet filled my nose as I entered the tiny waiting room and stepped up to the glass box housing the receptionist. "Can I help you?"

"Yes, I am here to apply for legal assistance with a divorce."

I could feel the weight of those words as they left my mouth. As she slid the clipboard and pen through the opening, the reality of what I was about to do hit me all at once. I am going to be a divorcee again. I never wanted to do this again! I never dreamed I would stand here in this smelly lobby filling out a sheet of paper for a stranger, explaining why I needed the divorce. I choked back tears.

Knowing what needed to be done, I took a deep breath and nervously started filling out the paperwork. I dreaded the land of courtrooms and lawyers, custody battles, and broken pieces of my dreams left scattered behind me. There was so much finality in this moment, but I knew it was the only way to get free of the abuse and heal.

It's very hard to heal a wound when the scab is constantly split back open. It's a painfully long process that can lead to infection. I couldn't heal if I kept allowing the wounds in my heart to take a beating. The wounds weren't even allowed time to scab over before new attacks came.

"Miss?" My thoughts were interrupted by the interviewer.

I sat down and slid the clipboard across the counter and under the plexiglass that separated her and I. Sitting in awkward silence as she read the paperwork; I fidgeted with my purse, trying to shove away my nervousness. Anxiety was threatening me as I waited. I focused on breathing.

In…out…in…out…*you're okay.* In…out…*God is with you.* In…out…in…out…*you are not alone.*

Finally, she spoke, "Can you elaborate on the things that occurred that you believe are abusive?" Not again! My thoughts raced.

I began with the greatest physical abuse, followed by the verbal and emotional abuse, concluding with the very reason I had to leave, the grand finale… not one, but two STDs. After sharing with her the recent text issues and what the abuse hotline advised me to do, she stood up and said, "Hold on one minute, please."

She exited her box and came around to where I was and invited me to join her in the back. She must have sensed my nervousness and assured me everything was okay. She only wanted me to meet someone that she believed could help. "Have a seat right here and Rachel will be right out to speak with you." She turned and hurriedly disappeared down the long hallway.

To my right sat a desk with papers scattered all over it and a computer. I noticed several filing cabinets lining the walls. I focused on the small trash can near my feet. I felt like I belonged in that tiny little can along with all the other discarded garbage from the day.

Finally, I heard footsteps and in walked Rachel. She took her seat and introduced herself to me. I sat, facing a woman about my age, completely bald, smiling from ear to ear with overwhelming love and acceptance in her eyes. She began by asking me questions about my situation and about my past. Some questions were the same as the ones I had just answered for the intake interview, but she was able to pull more details out of me.

As I listened to Rachel explain stats about how many times women go back into abusive relationships before they finally leave, I realized that there was no room for my victim mentality. I was staring into the face of a cancer patient who was helping me up out of the mud. Little did I know, Rachel would soon become one of my very dearest friends who God would use in ways that I would never have guessed when I first met her.

Rachel was a social worker and abuse advocate. She aided those who needed someone to guide them through the rocky terrain of restraining orders, strategizing a plan for escape, what to do after, and how to stay safe. She educated women about what abuse looks like and how to stop it… if they were ready.

After finding out where I was, she helped me formulate a plan to get the harassment to stop. All her advice, strategies, and information were so helpful and extremely comforting. I felt like I finally had someone in my corner who understood exactly what I was dealing with. Something about Rachel disarmed me. I felt as though I could share everything with her. It wasn't long before the thoughts of doubt I faced about my decisions came out. "I just don't know. What if I'm wrong? What if I am blowing this all out of proportion?"

I suppose I just wanted to be validated just one more time, but the truth was I really did battle going back and forth with myself. It was as if I were at war with my thoughts. I was so terrified of making the wrong choice in the past that it paralyzed me. Now that I was moving in what I hoped was the right direction, I needed to be assured that I wasn't barreling down the wrong track.

"Why are you seeking a divorce?" she asked.

"I'm afraid if I don't get a divorce, I'll go back." The words came tumbling out of my mouth.

She began rummaging through a filing cabinet nearby and laid a piece of paper in front of me with an image of a wheel. Directly in the center of the wheel were the following words: "Power and Control."

The wheel focused on eight different types of abuse tactics.[3]

As she shared what an unhealthy relationship looked like, it was no surprise to me that I had been caught in many of the spokes of that wheel. What was surprising was how blind I had been to the reality of it. I knew what was going on was wrong, and I wanted out, but I didn't know how. So, I threw up the blinders and ignored the issues.

After going through each area, Rachel asked, "How many of these areas have you experienced?" "All but one," I answered sadly as she flipped the paper over. There, on the other side, was a similar image, only this one was called the Equality Wheel.[4]

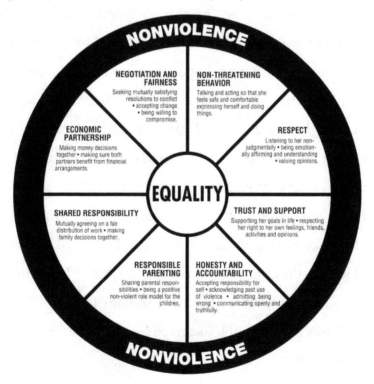

The Equality Wheel explained what a healthy, non-abusive relationship looked like.

As we read through the different areas of a healthy relationship, I grew even more sad. My thoughts drifted. *I knew it! I knew that's what it was supposed to look like. WHY? Why couldn't he just be normal?* Guess I'm not crazy after all. There it was in black and white! How can you argue with that? This was not an in-depth analysis, but it was more than enough for me to face the hard realization I had not experienced these healthy behaviors in my marriage.

I accepted poor treatment because not only did I devalue myself; I hated who I was. Going back through some of my journals from over a decade ago, I stumbled upon an entry that I couldn't finish reading. It began, *"I don't think it's possible to hate myself any more than I do right now. How can I hate myself this much?"* My heart grieved for my younger self as I gently closed the journal and thanked God for what He brought me out of.

How could I expect others to love me when I didn't even love myself? I accepted the abuse, believing that I deserved it. That was until I learned the truth of who I was as a daughter, adopted into the family of the One who created me. I couldn't love myself until I learned I was indeed lovable, deserved love, and was created to be loved. I was worthy of it!

Over the next few weeks, Rachel and I stayed in close contact, speaking almost every day. Her counsel was a vital asset to me in this season. She invested herself in my life with no expectation of anything in return. I learned valuable lessons from Rachel, starting with how to end the harassing text messages.

I was so frustrated one day after receiving a slew of texts, calling me every name in the book, insulting my parenting abilities, attacking my character and informing me I was going to hell if I divorced him. Even though I wasn't engaging with him, seeing the messages was frustrating and infuriating. After listening to me go on about how exhausting they were to read, she simply replied, "Well, just don't read them."

"I don't want to read them, but what if there is something that was actually important in one and I missed it?"

She said, "Just screenshot them without reading them and send them all to me. I will read them and if there is something important you need to know, I will definitely tell you."

I cannot even explain the weight that fell off my shoulders the next day when those messages came in and I didn't read a single word! I simply did what I was told, and peace replaced the chaos. Drama eliminated!

ANOTHER WAY

Unfortunately, I was denied legal aid as they could only take a few cases and mine was not high enough on the list. At first, it devastated me, wondering how I would ever afford a divorce attorney. Thankfully, I'd learned to take those cares to God and wait on Him. I was now fully certain divorce was necessary for legal reasons and for my safety. After separating, things only spiraled more out of control for Jerry. The poor choices that were being made while living together only escalated. As long as we were legally married, he deemed me his property, identity included.

God knew all of this. He knew the things that happened that were too atrocious to even write about. Even knowing how much God hates divorce, I was certain He hated the mistreatment of His children even more. The day I found out I wouldn't be getting financial help with my divorce was an opportunity for me to put into practice all I had learned about the faithfulness of God. The old "chicken without a head" routine wouldn't work this time. After many nights of journaling my thoughts and hearing God in my quiet times, I rested on this.

Things don't always go the way I picture or the way I think they should. If I kept trying to make things happen, I would miss out on God's best for me. His timing is better and His ways are higher than mine. He sees the bigger picture and can piece things together for my good and His glory. I only needed to release my grip on the problem, lay down my need to control, rest, and be content to let Him lead.

I learned to trust God by taking inventory of how He cared for me and by spending time getting to know Him. This meant turning off my TV, smartphone, computer or whatever else was causing me to numb out and ignore the Creator of the Universe. He was the only one who could bring about true freedom from the pain of the past and remove the lies planted in my soul. He wanted me to know the truth of His promises so that I could be unshakeable when the storms of life came. He was calling me into my destiny and placing within me a desire for the things He desired.

During this season of great change and healing, I only wanted to be with God. I longed for our time together. I had an urgency to stay connected as I battled depression and overwhelming heartbreak. I was fully aware that without Him, I wouldn't make it. I went from being co-dependent longing for independence to realizing I only needed to be God-dependent.

The words, "You'll never make it without me. You'll have nothing, you'll be nothing and you can do nothing," that I so often heard changed. Anytime I remembered those awful words spoken over me, I replaced the word "me" with the word "God" and the power of those words shifted. What was once discouraging and painful became empowering. It's wonderful knowing that I needed only to rely on God. It was through Him that I was something and I could do anything. It was because of God that I would have anything!

I knew worrying about how I was going to get the legal steps taken care of to protect myself were no longer my concern. I didn't know how, but I knew He is a God of impossible and makes a way when there is no way, and He did!

21

THE GREAT PHYSICIAN

During the divorce, I began seeing a counselor at my church to help me process what I was experiencing so that I could take back my life. This was a hard step for me because I still battled the fear of being judged because of what I was going through. I already struggled with feeling like I was an outsider. Now, to make matters worse, I imagined I had the word "DIVORCEE" pasted on my forehead. I was certain anyone who walked by me knew and thought I should be ashamed of myself. Even though God understood, was fully aware of the situation, and was not disappointed in me, I convinced myself everyone else was.

Any hopes of my life ever being used as an example to lead others had vanished. How could God use the mess I was in and the outcome to glorify His name? How could I work for a church and be going through a divorce? I wondered how long before I would receive the letter asking me to quietly resign from my position. These were the very questions I began my first counseling session asking. I used up forty-five minutes of our hour together by revealing my deepest concerns about what others think of me and the certain doom of my witness!

Darlene listened patiently as I rambled on and when I finished, she assured me of two things: God loves me and will never turn His back on me and that God's family loved me and would never cast me out. She tore down the lie that I was the only one who had issues and that others were judging me. The shame I believed others were projecting onto me wasn't from them, but from the one who accuses day and night, the enemy of my soul (Revelations 12:10). Chances were they didn't know a thing! Chances were even higher that if they knew, they prayed for me without judgment and loved me as I was.

So, with that behind me, healing could begin. I pursued healing during the process instead of waiting until the divorce was over and I was left searching for my missing limbs. I never expected it to be easy. I was sure it would be tough and painful, but I was determined to walk out in one piece, no matter what.

The night before my second counseling session, I sat staring at a blank journal page, frustrated and angry that things were so hard. I wanted to throw whatever would fit into the back of my car, buckle up my children, drive as far away as possible, and never look back. I knew running away wouldn't solve anything, and the truth was, I couldn't run away from myself or the one who attacked my identity day and night. I had to stand and fight. I had to forgive to be free from resentment and anger, but I didn't know how to.

As I cried out in desperation to the Lord, I wrote: *"Father, I have battled the enemy over my identity for far too long. I asked you to do something big and rearrange my heart and life. Use me like a steady arrow. Just shoot me in the right direction. I've asked you to use my life to leave a footprint and make a difference... to be different. I don't want average and ordinary. I want brave and bold. That is who you say I am. You brought me here and I know you will not leave me. I desire to walk in forgiveness and to make room for you to move, but I have been so badly wounded. I know I can't walk in the fullness of all you have for me if I don't release Jerry to you and forgive, BUT I DON'T KNOW HOW! Help me, God! You know all he's done..."*

I listed everything that came to mind that he'd ever done to cause me the greatest pain, hoping writing it would help me release those events. When I finished, one and a half pages later, sorrow overcame me, and I wept. How could I ever be free from this pain? I lay in silence, waiting for sleep.

By morning, sorrow turned to disgust. I still had no idea how I was supposed to forgive. Now, not only was I mad at Jerry for everything he'd done that hurt me, I was angry at myself for allowing it to go on for so long. I stared into the mirror, wishing I could just let it all go.

Later that afternoon, I shared with Darlene my desire to walk in forgiveness and my struggle to do so. At the end of the session, she handed me a thin little book by June Hunt called *Forgiveness-The Freedom to Let Go*, and instructed me to go through it slowly, allowing God to speak to my heart in each section. I knew I couldn't forgive the extensive laundry list of wrongs on my own and wasn't sure how reading a book would make it any easier. Expressing my deep concern that I would fail; she shared an analogy with me that forever changed the way I viewed God the Great Physician (John 5:1-9).

Darlene was diagnosed with breast cancer and ultimately needed a double mastectomy. To prepare for the surgery, a myriad of things had to be done by a team of medical professionals. She didn't just walk in and go straight to the operating table. Once she was clear to enter the operating room, she had to choose to get on the operating table herself. No one forced her onto the table. It was her choice to lie down and submit her body to the surgeon. She trusted the skill of the surgeon to remove the cancer from her body.

In the same way, God is our surgeon, skilled in gently removing anything that doesn't belong that's causing sickness and disease. I could choose to submit my will to His skill and let Him operate on my heart, removing the pain of the past and unforgiveness.

Similarly, I needed to prep before entering the operating room to get on the operating table under the care of The Great Physician. I had to lie down my pride and realize that I couldn't remove my own tumor. I said yes to spending the time it would take to go through the physical therapy that would be required afterwards. Once I was fully committed and submitted, I rested, knowing I was only responsible to do what I can do. God will take care of the rest.

A week later, I had a phone conversation with Rachel, my abuse advocate. I was sharing some bad dreams I was having because of the way Jerry was treating the children and the heartache they were experiencing. These waters were uncharted and, watching my kids hurt in this new way, enraged me. I explained that I'd started writing the things down that I held against him and, one at a time, released them verbally to God.

After listening to the situation and how I was dealing with it, she said, "It seems like you are on the operating table, just like I will be soon for my double mastectomy and reconstruction. My surgeon is specifically skilled to deal with my condition. God is like a surgeon, capable of dealing with your pain. He is skilled at removing the infected tissue and replacing what is missing with something new and wonderful. It can be a painful process but on the other side is healing."

God, you have my full attention now! He was confirming His character and His promises to me daily.

These women God placed in my life to help me through my pain were breast cancer survivors. My counselor and abuse advocate were both just on the other side of beating it. This was no small coincidence. I believe God was showing me strong women who had great pain and overcame what the enemy meant for their destruction. They overcame with faith greater than their fear, relying on the one who heals to do exactly what He promises. They refused to hold on to bitterness in their diagnosis and trusted God would take care of each step.

I wasn't fighting physical cancer, but I was indeed fighting a type of cancer. One that affected not only my spiritual and mental health, but, if left unchecked, my physical health as well. Holding onto unforgiveness is like drinking poison and expecting the offender to die. Ultimately, it doesn't hurt them, but it can kill us.

Forgiveness matters and can be accomplished no matter how large or small the offense. It is only one choice away, but there are several steps that can be taken to get there. The first step is always the same; a willingness to release the offense and trust God for your justice. I didn't know how, but I knew I wanted to live in peace and have joy. With that in mind, I said yes to God and let him walk with me on my journey to forgive the unforgivable.

Viewing God as my surgeon was exactly what I needed to release myself from the full weight of responsibility. Just like Darlene and Rachel couldn't have cut off their own body parts, neither could I cut out my bitterness. I followed Darlene's counsel and started reading my little forgiveness book, taking notes everywhere I felt prompted. I slowly went through each section, soaking in what God says about forgiveness and the high cost of holding onto it.

I journaled, "*God, give me courage to release resentment. Help me to be free from bitterness and anger. I don't want to hold on to it to feel justified. It's far too heavy! For so long, I have felt like a plastic bag tossed in the wind, going back and forth wherever the wind blew me. I'm ready to land, to be still and know that you are God and you got this! You got me! I release my burdens to you. I trust you with my heart and believe you are the Great Physician, skilled to remove every infected area. Heal every part of my body and mind that has experienced trauma. Fear has no place here. I choose to stand in faith that You are who You say You are and will do what You say You'll do!*"

This was a process and many times, the things I would forgive one day would creep back in on another. Sometimes, I had to forgive the same thing every ten minutes. I knew I hadn't truly forgiven the offense if I still felt anger, followed by thoughts of revenge. So, I would go to my surgeon again and again.

"Lord, I am so sorry for the unforgiveness in my heart. I am angry at Jerry, but right now I release him to you again. I give you full permission into areas of my life where I am hiding unforgiveness, even unknowingly. God, help me forgive the unforgivable… the wrongs that have left me feeling justified to be angry and unforgiving. I have taken your rightful place as judge. Forgive me God. Help me forgive those who have wronged me. You will defend me and do a much better job than I could, so I give up my seat and give you back Yours.

Have you forsaken the weak or downtrodden? No, you have defended the poor and oppressed, brought healing to the weak, sick and broken (Psalm 82:3). You said, blessed are those who mourn, for the kingdom of Heaven is theirs (Matthew 5:4). You are near to the broken-hearted (Psalm 34:18) and I feel you so close to me. Heal my wounds!

Thank you for loving me and adopting me as your own. For wooing me, for calling me, for seeing me. I am on the operating table right now and you are the skilled surgeon with steady hands, slowly peeling away the layers of death, rot, and stink. You are taking away the old and bringing forth new. Never moving too quickly or too slowly, but perfectly."

For much of life, I felt like I was in a desert; wandering, thirsty, dry and alone. Many times, I wasn't sure I could go on anymore. I didn't yet know that what the enemy meant for evil, God would use for good (Genesis 50:20). He was working behind the scenes, orchestrating something wonderful if I would be patient.

My children and I would be taken care of and I could trust that God had my best interest in mind (Jeremiah 29:11). He knew everything I needed before I even knew I needed it (Matthew 6:8). I had learned to be like the flower in the field that never worries about what it's going to wear and the birds who never wonder what they're going to eat because God provides all that they need, and they trust him (Matthew 6:26-30).

I am chosen and valuable. I am free, secure, loved, forgiven, and complete. I am His.

22

THIS IS NOT THE END, ITS ONLY THE BEGINNING

I lived so much of my life, captured behind the walls of fear, bound by the lies of the enemy. Satan's plan was that I never discover the truth of my real identity. He worked so hard to keep me isolated and separated so that I would not learn of God's great love or the victory I was designed to live in.

I didn't choose abuse when I was a little girl. There was nothing I believed I could do about it. The message the abuse sent to my heart about who I am and what I deserve in life led me to accept abuse as an adult. These experiences formed my internal belief system through which I viewed myself, the world, and God. All were distorted.

Painful things happen that have the ability to leave us feeling disappointed, discouraged, and disillusioned. These events can stick with us, weighing down, and exhausting us to keep us weak. Maybe you were born into poverty, suffered terrible loss, illness, abuse, neglect or other trauma. We wonder, where is God in this? Satan offers us an explanation; God must not be good, and neither are we. If God were good, He wouldn't let these things happen to us.

Then, not only is our view of ourselves skewed, our view of God gets distorted as well. Satan's main goal is to separate us from all truth. The Word of God calls him the father of lies in John 8:44. He has been doing it from the beginning of humanity. He challenged God's instructions and His goodness in the Garden when tempting Eve. By introducing a lie, he caused her to doubt that what God said was true.

"And the woman said to the serpent, 'We may eat of the fruit of the trees in the garden, but God said, 'You shall not eat of the fruit of the tree that is in the midst of the garden, neither shall you touch it, lest you die.' But the serpent said to the woman, 'You will not surely die. For God knows that when you eat of it, your eyes will be opened, and you will be like God, knowing good and evil'" (Genesis 3:2-5 NIV).

She believed God was withholding His best from her. With one tiny idea suggested by the enemy, she doubted God's instructions and His character. As she exchanged the truth for a lie, she saw herself fully exposed, ashamed, and unworthy. Now, instead of running to God, she ran away.

It has never been God's desire for any of us to be held captive by the lies of the enemy and live bound by the chains of sin. This could be our own sin or the result of someone else's. However, God gave humanity the gift of choice even when He knew not everyone was going to choose Him. We were created for relationship with God and real relationship and true love is never forced.

He loved us so much that through the sacrifice of Jesus, there's now a way for us to live in close relationship with Him again. Because of the blood of Jesus, He no longer sees the old, sinful version but rather, a new, pure version without spot or blemish (2 Corinthians 5:17). We can enter into His wonderful promises of provision and protection if we believe and know who we are IN Christ Jesus.

It is God's desire that we live in freedom as we walk out this life fully aware of our identity in Christ. If we don't believe we are created to love and be loved, that we are created intentionally and not by mistake, if we don't know we are sons and daughters of God through Christ Jesus, then we are a victim of mistaken identity. If we don't know who we are, then we're more likely to believe the lie that we were not created with a purpose, on purpose.

I believed I was sentenced to a life of isolation, fear, rejection, pain, and loneliness. I believed there was nothing beyond the darkness of my confines. A lie cannot be exposed if it hides in the dark. Identity is established based on our belief systems. What we behold, we become (2 Corinthians 3:18). If we are always looking at what the enemy says about us, then that is who we believe we are. To find out who we really are and what we are capable of, we must choose to answer the voice calling out, "OVER HERE! Look this way! The gate is open. There is life on this side. Freedom is waiting!" The Word of God brings light to the dark places and exposes the lies.

Even after I discovered the gate was open to escape my proverbial prison camp, I was leery of leaving. Venturing into the unknown was scary. Once I was brave enough to take a step outside the walls of fear, I panicked and ran back inside. I'd never been outside the walls. What if it was even worse? Curiosity kept me hanging around the gate and toying with ideas about what it would be like to live free. I heard a voice on the other side saying, "trust me," and sharing of a new way of life. One I'd only dreamed of. I tried to leave several more times and each time I got further before running back to the familiar barriers. Eventually, I stopped at the gate to consider the ramifications of staying this way. What if I were meant for more? I took a deep breath, kicked it open, and ran full force into the unknown, never looking back.

Learning to live on the other side of the lies has been a process. It took time to learn a new way of living. But God never left me to figure it out on my own. Healing was my primary focus for quite some time. Healing my mind and my heart.

After a while, I finally felt at home in my newfound freedom. Eventually I settled into my new identity, Kathryn Rose, meaning pure flower. I spent time learning the ways of a daughter. I rested under the covering of my Husband—Father God until it was time to get up and move on to the next destination.

> "For your Maker is your husband, the Lord of hosts is his name; and the Holy One of Israel is your Redeemer, the God of the whole earth he is called." (Isaiah 54:5 ESV)

DISCOVERING TRUTH

Once I believed the truth about who I was, it canceled out the lies. I don't believe I would have ever discovered these truths on my own. I needed the guidance of others to point me in the right direction and pick me up when I tripped over my victim mentality. Sure, I had access to the tools, but my problem was I didn't know how to use them. In case you might feel the same way, don't worry, I got you!

I created a poster of verses from the Word declaring 'Who I Am' and hung it on the wall in my bathroom. I need to see it every day to continuously reject the lies that try to come. I've included it in the back of this book for you as a starting point and for quick reference. This is not an exhaustive list, but it's a great start! I know that if I don't have my weaponry ready, I can't fight and the Word is sharper than any two-edge sword (Hebrews 4:12).

When I've had a rough day or just feel discouraged, I take a break from life, lock the bathroom door and read my poster. I walk away feeling taller, hopeful and reminded that I am seen, chosen and loved. It puts my eyes back on that which I am becoming! I am no longer looking at myself "as is" or focusing my gaze on the trying circumstances of life. I am refocusing and beholding the truth of how God sees me through Christ.

Unfortunately, we can't always help what others do to us or how we're treated, especially as a child, but we can learn the truth about who we are and our identity by seeking what He says about us. The only way to know this is by spending time in the Word and reading the truth for ourselves. Then not only by reading but speaking it out loud so that we can create new pathways to truth in our mind. There is something powerful about hearing what God says about us out of our own mouth.

When I began getting to know Jesus, I spent time with Him the same way you do when you first meet the love of your life. I soaked up every moment we shared. I thought of Him throughout my day, and the closer I got to Jesus, the more I saw Him in my reflection. Being in His presence will cause you to step into truth and discover who you really are. Your true identity.

To walk out of the enemy's camp, we must know who we are and to whom we belong. We can bring our brokenness and pain to Jesus, trusting He knows how to handle it. The beatings of this life may have left us weak, but once we discover truth, we can exchange the lie that because we are weak, we're useless. Paul, one of the most zealous men on fire for the gospel in his day, spoke of his weakness. Satan sent a messenger to harass him while he shared the truth of Christ with his generation.

Paul was on assignment from God, knew who he was in Christ, and was even filled with the Holy Spirit, yet he knew he was weak. The things in this world were beating him down; exhausting, distracting and attempting to make him quit! When Paul petitioned the Lord, asking this "thorn be removed from his side," the Lord responded, "My grace is sufficient for you, for my power is made perfect in weakness." I can imagine Paul shouting praise as he grabbed this truth. I picture him dancing around in circles and shouting, "I will boast all the more gladly of my weaknesses, so that the power of Christ may rest upon me. For the sake of Christ, then, I am content with weaknesses, insults, hardships, persecutions and calamities. For when I am weak, then I am strong" (2 Corinthians 12:7-10).

It was as if Paul shouted in the devil's face, "Go, ahead! Hit me with your best shot." Paul knew he was much better off allowing the power of Christ to rest on him like armor. It was then that he was made strong and could handle the attack of the enemy via hardship, persecution, and calamity.

In John 16:33, Jesus tells us, "In this life there will be trouble, but take heart for I have overcome the world" (NIV). He is letting us know up front, "Hey, things are going to be tough, but don't worry or be afraid, I got you." None of us gets out of this life unscathed. There will be hard things to deal with. Wounds will come. No matter the level of pain or heartbreak you have experienced or will experience, God promises, "The Lord himself goes before you and will be with you; he will never leave you nor forsake you..." and then He commands us, "Do not be afraid; do not be discouraged" (Deuteronomy 31:8 NIV). Trust God with your pain and hurt. Let him heal your wounds. He is your strength and will uphold you with His righteous right hand (Isaiah 41:10).

KEEP YOUR EYES ON JESUS

Our wounds draw the enemy like a predator who has gotten a whiff of the scent of blood. Satan tries to intimidate us in the area where we are most wounded. He whispers and sometimes shouts lies to get us to take our eyes off Jesus and onto our pain and problems. This is why I created my bathroom poster!

We need to acknowledge we have a real enemy, but then be careful not to give him our full attention. When the storm is raging all around us and we're in the middle of deep water, we must stay focused on the truth of Jesus or risk drowning. How do we keep our eyes on Jesus when the storms of life are so loud and scary? How can we keep our gaze on His face and not on the wind and waves threatening to overtake us?

A practical way I have found is to keep saying who God is in my situation. To remind myself that my healing is a process and I am moving toward the promise of victory. I must remind myself of who HE says HE is first, then who He says I am.

"Blessed are those who trust in the Lord and have made the Lord their hope and confidence." (Jeremiah 17:7 NLT)

I list out His promises, pick one or two that anchor me in that seasonal storm and stand firmly planted on those until it passes and it always passes. However, I don't come out on the other side left unchanged. I don't come out looking like a beaten or broken vessel, but instead, I am stronger and more like Him.

Isaiah 54:11 says, "Oh, afflicted one, storm tossed and not comforted. Behold, I will set your stones in antimony. I will lay your foundation in sapphires" (ESV).

When I discovered this verse, I saw myself as the "afflicted, storm tossed one." The smoothest stones are the ones beaten by raging waters, and just as David chose smooth stones to bring down the enemy, God chose me to bring down generational strongholds.

His love called me by name; Victorious, Valuable Daughter. He showed me how to live free in the joy of the Lord. He gave me His peace that would bring stillness to the raging waters of my tormented mind. God's love sees everything and still loves.

When I was in His presence, I knew I was seen. There wasn't anything I could say to God that would surprise Him. He already knew. He knew I didn't trust Him and why. He knew I was afraid and why. He knew I was ashamed... and He knew why. Once I recognized the truth of God's love, the fear of judgment was gone. I held tight to the truth that I was covered in the blood of Christ and my sins were forgiven. Where there is truth, there is freedom!

A NOTE FROM THE AUTHOR

THE REST OF THE STORY

I've always had a way of making people feel comfortable enough around me to share very personal things. People I don't even know begin unloading their deepest concerns within a few moments of a conversation. It has been this way for me since I was a kid. Somehow, I was the "advice girl" for my friends and family. I really can't tell you why. I didn't have all the answers. I just listened. One thing I have learned is that everyone has issues! We just want to be heard and to know we are not alone.

We all have a story, a past, a history. And no matter how disturbing it may seem; your story needs to be told. Someone else may hear it and realize they are not alone in their struggles. The Word tells us we will overcome by the blood of the lamb and the WORD of our TESTIMONY (Revelation 12:11). So, speak up! Share what's happened and how God's shown up for you, even if you haven't already arrived at whatever perfect ending you imagine life to have. Just a heads up, there isn't one. Not this side of Heaven, at least.

Something beautiful happens when we open up and share our story. We encourage those around us and remind ourselves of all that God has done in our life and how far He has brought us. That is how we avoid the traps the enemy plants for us to fall into. When we use our voice to bring God glory in our story, His-story, then we stomp on the enemy's head!

When I have shared my story with those I meet, it is usually met with shock. Knowing we all have a past is one thing, realizing what that past is, is a whole different ball game. We see a snapshot of someone's life and think, "Wow, they've got it all together." The big picture is always much more unraveled than we imagine.

It has not always been easy to share my story. There have been times I have wanted to cover it all up and ignore it happened. The attack on my life has been great, but the attack on my voice has been greater. Satan has done so much to try to keep me quiet. He knows there is power in our story.

I've been afraid to speak up since I was a little girl. The gatekeepers to my freedom and the freedom of those around me were named Guilt and Shame. They were always ready to remind me why I should hide and be quiet.

As a little girl, I tried to scream when I was being harmed and couldn't. As I aged, I learned to be quiet, to not cause conflict and protect myself. Ten years ago, when I realized the power of our testimony, my voice began being attacked in my sleep. I had dreams where I would try to rescue someone or myself from peril. I knew that all would be well if I could only say the name of Jesus. Yet when I opened my mouth, nothing would come out, no matter how hard I tried. At other times, I've woken from sleep to the feeling of someone chocking the breath out of me and could not scream for help. No one is there, but I can't open my mouth for a moment. Like it's glued shut. I've learned to recognize the tactics the enemy uses. It's nothing new.

Our voice is a threat because we use it to share the love of Jesus with those around us. We can speak and make mountains move (Mark 11:23). We can encourage, build up, and heal others with our voice. I've decided to share my story before I've arrived at "Perfect Station" because I've realized it doesn't exist. I've been healed of so much and I am still being healed. I am a work in progress. My story isn't over yet, it is only just beginning.

As I write the words of this part of my story, I have been free from the bondage of abuse for six years. I am now happily married to my best friend James and we've added another arrow in our quiver who is just about to turn three. There was so much healing that took place before I was even open to the prospect of getting married again. I can remember telling God I was done with men and content to live alone for the rest of my life, and I meant it.

Shortly after I said that, my oldest son invited me to attend a tennis match with my daughter and one of his mentors, who was a man named James. I was honored he wanted me to attend and even though I had never played tennis in my life; I agreed to go. James, my children, and I laughed and played for over four hours that day. I decided since he was mentoring my son, I should get to know him better. There was something unique about him. I soon found myself attracted to him without warning! He was gentle, soft spoken, patient, kind and smiled all the time! I realized what I was drawn to the most was God in him.

He had a beautiful understanding of God's love for him and He loved God. I was sure if He could love God that much, he would love me well. I knew he was "the one" when he asked me out on our first date. He took me to a prophetic teaching night at a friend's church. One year later, we were married.

Life looks very different for me now. I am so thankful for that. But marrying my best friend didn't magically fix everything. I still had to do all the heavy lifting to get healed up front. I don't believe I could have received love the way God intended me to until I walked through forgiveness and released my bitterness. I would have never opened up to trusting another man if I didn't first learn to trust God and listen to His voice. I ferociously went after my healing, determined I would not be a victim anymore. I was going to walk healed and in the victory I was created for.

—*Kathryn Rose*

SCRIPTURES ON IDENTITY

Use the following verses as a starting point to help you see yourself the way God does. Start declaring each scripture over yourself every day for one week. Look them up and declare it from the pages of scripture if you like.

Declare them out loud. Whispering or shout them forcefully if you need to. Then sit down and journal about what effect you've experienced.

Engage your heart with them: don't let them just be words. Recognize that you're speaking to both all of Heaven and all of hell when you're announcing these truths.

The King Decrees This Day that I am....

- I am complete in Him Who is the Head of all principality and power (Colossians 2:10).
- I am alive with Christ (Ephesians 2:5).
- I am free from the law of sin and death (Romans 8:2).
- I am far from oppression, and fear does not come near me (Isaiah 54:14).
- I am born of God, and the evil one does not touch me (1 John 5:18).
- I am holy and without blame before Him in love (Ephesians 1:4; 1 Peter 1:16).
- I have the mind of Christ (1 Corinthians 2:16; Philippians 2:5).
- I have the peace of God that passes all understanding (Philippians 4:7).
- I have the Greater One living in me; greater is He Who is in me than he who is in the world (1 John 4:4).
- I have received the gift of righteousness and reign as a king in life by Jesus Christ (Romans 5:17).
- I have received the spirit of wisdom and revelation in the knowledge of Jesus, the eyes of my understanding being enlightened (Ephesians 1:17-18).
- I have received the power of the Holy Spirit to lay hands on the sick and see them recover, to cast out demons, to speak with new tongues. I have power over all the power of the enemy, and nothing shall by any means harm me (Mark 16:17-18; Luke 10:17-19).

- I have put off the old man and have put on the new man, which is renewed in the knowledge after the image of Him Who created me (Colossians 3:9-10).
- I have given, and it is given to me; good measure, pressed down, shaken together, and running over, men give into my bosom (Luke 6:38).
- I have no lack for my God supplies all of my need according to His riches in glory by Christ Jesus (Philippians 4:19).
- I can quench all the fiery darts of the wicked one with my shield of faith (Ephesians 6:16).
- I can do all things through Christ Jesus (Philippians 4:13).
- I show forth the praises of God Who has called me out of darkness into His marvelous light (1 Peter 2:9).
- I am God's child for I am born again of the incorruptible seed of the Word of God, which lives and abides forever (1 Peter 1:23).
- I am God's workmanship, created in Christ unto good works (Ephesians 2:10).
- I am a new creature in Christ (2 Corinthians 5:17).
- I am a spirit being alive to God (Romans 6:11; Thessalonians 5:23).
- I am a believer, and the light of the Gospel shines in my mind (2 Corinthians 4:4).
- I am a doer of the Word and blessed in my actions (James 1:22,25).
- I am a joint-heir with Christ (Romans 8:17).

- I am more than a conqueror through Him Who loves me (Romans 8:37).
- I am an overcomer by the blood of the Lamb and the word of my testimony (Revelation 12:11).
- I am a partaker of His divine nature (2 Peter 1:3-4).
- I am an ambassador for Christ (2 Corinthians 5:20).
- I am part of a chosen generation, a royal priesthood, a holy nation, a purchased people (1 Peter 2:9).
- I am the righteousness of God in Jesus Christ (2 Corinthians 5:21).
- I am the temple of the Holy Spirit; I am not my own (1 Corinthians 6:19).
- I am the head and not the tail; I am above only and not beneath (Deuteronomy 28:13).
- I am the light of the world (Matthew 5:14).
- I am His elect, full of mercy, kindness, humility, and long suffering (Romans 8:33; Colossians 3:12).
- I am forgiven of all my sins and washed in the Blood (Ephesians 1:7).
- I am delivered from the power of darkness and translated into God's kingdom (Colossians 1:13).
- I am redeemed from the curse of sin, sickness, and poverty (Deuteronomy 28:15-68; Galatians 3:13).
- I am firmly rooted, built up, established in my faith and overflowing with gratitude (Colossians 2:7).
- I am called of God to be the voice of His praise (Psalm 66:8; 2 Timothy 1:9).

- I am healed by the stripes of Jesus (Isaiah 53:5; 1 Peter 2:24).
- I am raised up with Christ and seated in heavenly places (Ephesians 2:6; Colossians 2:12).
- I am greatly loved by God (Romans 1:7; Ephesians 2:4; Colossians 3:12; 1 Thessalonians 1:4).
- I am strengthened with all might according to His glorious power (Colossians 1:11).
- I am submitted to God, and the devil flees from me because I resist him in the Name of Jesus (James 4:7).
- I press on toward the goal to win the prize to which God in Christ Jesus is calling us upward (Philippians 3:14).
- For God has not given us a spirit of fear; but of power, love, and a sound mind (2 Timothy 1:7).
- It is not I who live, but Christ lives in me (Galatians 2:20).

ABOUT AUTHOR

Kathryn May has been in ministry for ten years advocating for women to discover the truth of who they are in Christ. She is a Certified Mental Health Coach through the Association of Christian Counselors and desires to help others overcome the pain of the past and live with peace and freedom.

Kathryn runs a YouTube channel to share her journey to living healthy from the inside out. She currently resides in Tennessee, is married to the love of her life, James, and together they parent three amazing miracles.

Kathryn Rose May

Whole | Healed | Healthy

▶ www.youtube.com/kathrynmay

f Ⓞ Kathryn Rose May

www.kathrynrosemay.com

ENDNOTES

Chapter 8
(1) Walker, L. E. (1979). *The battered woman. New York: Harper & Row.*

Chapter 11
(2) Walker, Tom. *"How Thomas Edison's Mother Was The Making of Him…" Legends Report, 24 May 2020, www.legends.report/how-thomas-edisons-mother-was-the-making-of-him/.*

Chapter 21
(3) *"The Power and Control Wheel (The Duluth Model)." Free Social Work Tools and Resources: SocialWorkersToolbox.com, 29 Sept. 2018, www.socialworkerstoolbox.com/the-power-and-control-wheel-the-duluth-model/.*

(4) *"The Equality Wheel (The Duluth Model)." Free Social Work Tools and Resources: SocialWorkersToolbox.com, 29 Sept. 2018, http://www.socialworkerstoolbox.com/the-equality-wheel-the-duluth-model/.*

CPSIA information can be obtained
at www.ICGtesting.com
Printed in the USA
BVHW091343140921
616733BV00012B/320